# Colorado Rockies 2019

## A Baseball Companion

*Edited by Patrick Dubuque, Aaron Gleeman and Bret Sayre*

Baseball Prospectus

**Craig Brown and Dave Pease, Consultant Editors**
**Rob McQuown and Harry Pavlidis, Statistics Editors**

Copyright © 2019 by DIY Baseball, LLC.
All rights reserved

This book or any part thereof may not be reproduced or transmitted in any form or by any means, electronic or mechanical, including photocopying, recording, or by any information storage and retrieval system, without permission in writing from the publisher.

Limit of Liability/Disclaimer of Warranty: While the publisher and the author have used their best efforts in preparing this book, they make no representations or warranties with respect to the accuracy or completeness of the contents of this book and specifically disclaim any implied warranties of merchantability or fitness for a particular purpose. No warranty may be created or extended by sales representatives or written sales materials. The advice and strategies contained herein may not be suitable for your situation. You should consult with a professional where appropriate. Neither the publisher nor the author shall be liable for any loss of profit or any other commercial damages, including but not limited to special, incidental, consequential, or other damages.

Library of Congress Cataloging-in-Publication Data:
paperback
ISBN-13: 978-1-949332-38-4

Project Credits
Cover Design: Kathleen Dyson
Interior Design and Production: Jeff Pease, Dave Pease
Layout: Jeff Pease, Dave Pease

Baseball icon courtesy of Uberux, from https://www.shareicon.net/author/uberux

Ballpark diagram courtesy of Lou Spirito/THIRTY81 Project, https://thirty81project.com/

Manufactured in the United States of America
10 9 8 7 6 5 4 3 2 1

# Table of Contents

Foreword .................................................. v
    *Rob Mains*

Statistical Introduction ................................... vii

## Part 1: Team Analysis

Table for Two: Previewing the 2019 Colorado Rockies ............... 3
    *Jen Mac Ramos and Jeffrey Paternostro*

Performance Graphs ............................................ 7

2018 Team Performance ......................................... 8

2019 Team Projections ......................................... 9

Team Personnel ............................................... 10

Coors Field Stats ............................................ 11

Rockies Team Analysis ........................................ 13

## Part 2: Player Analysis

Rockies Player Analysis ...................................... 18

Rockies Prospects ............................................ 93

## Part 3: Featured Articles

The Hole in The Shift is Fixing Itself ...................... 107
    *Russell Carleton*

The State of the Quality Start .............................. 111
    *Rob Mains*

Heads-Up Hacking—The First Pitch ............................ 117
    *Matthew Trueblood*

A Hymn for the Index Stat ................................... 123
    *Patrick Dubuque*

Index of Names .............................................. 127

# Foreword

## Rob Mains

Welcome to this companion of the 2019 Colorado Rockies. We at Baseball Prospectus are excited to provide this analysis of the Rockies.

Our website, Baseball Prospectus, is a leader in delivering high-quality commentary and data to baseball fans everywhere. To some, those words—commentary and data—appear mutually exclusive. There are people out there who believe that traditional analysis and advanced analytics must run on different paths. But the simplistic narrative of stats vs. traditionalists just isn't true. Every team's analytics department interacts with scouting, development, and major league operations with a common goal: Delivering a championship. New technologies, like radar tracking of pitch speeds and movement, enable talent evaluators to focus on qualitative aspects of pitching like mechanics and pitch sequencing. In-game strategies like infield shifts, based on batters' hit tendencies, help turn balls in play into outs. Hitters use information to adjust their swings to maximize run production.

All these numbers can seem, at best, intimidating, and at worst, counterproductive to the casual fan. Even as technology and analysis have embedded themselves deeply into the way teams run, it can often feel like statistics create a displacement between the viewer and the sport, breaking them out of the action. And yet every fan incorporates the numbers to some degree; stats like batting average and earned run average, so fundamental to how we talk about performance, are actually complicated formulas. They don't bother people because those formulas have become second nature, as easy to translate as the action on the field.

Along the way, new statistics have entered baseball's lexicon. You'll see some of them, like on-base percentage (which measures a batter's ability to get on base via walk, hit batter, or hit), OPS (on-base plus slugging), and average exit velocity (the speed of balls off a hitter's bat) on broadcasts. Others, like DRC+, might well be new to you. Some of them have been well-defined to the public, others haven't. That lack of context has created ambiguity. Fans know that a ball hit 100 mph is scorched, but does that mean extra bases? (Not if it's hit on the ground or high in the air it doesn't.)

For those who are amenable to them, the new statistics can increase the enjoyment and understanding of the game. They can help fans identify when a pitcher is tiring, when a stolen base or a bunt attempt makes sense (and, more often, when it doesn't), or how a team's lineup might be constructed. Websites like Baseball Prospectus add to that understanding by weaving metrics into the narrative of the game. That's the goal of this publication: to take some of the newer, more complicated statistics and make them as intuitive as the ones on the back of old baseball cards.

But you don't need to love analytics to love baseball. The fans at BP who worked together to write this guide are captivated first and foremost by the game itself. We're drawn to Aaron Judge's power, Francisco Lindor's glove, Billy Hamilton's speed and Patrick Corbin's slider and don't need numbers to tell us why they're so mesmerizing. The underlying statistics provide depth to the game that we all love.

We hope you'll find that this guide helps you better understand the Rockies. Our analysts have studied the team's major league personnel and its minor league affiliates to identify their strengths and weaknesses, both the obvious ones and those that only a careful dissection of players' performances—yes, including the data—can reveal. You don't need us to tell you who was good and who wasn't in 2018, but our models and writers can help you project how each player is going to perform this year and beyond, and appreciate the greatness of each new game as it unfolds. As in the sport itself, the human and analytic components combine to generate a deeper overall understanding.

Think back to the first time you saw a baseball game on a high-definition TV. You'd grown familiar with how the game looked and felt on a picture tube. But new TV allowed you to see details that you'd never seen before. That's how advanced statistics work. The game itself is why you're here and why you're buying this. (And, for that matter, why we wrote it.) The statistical measures provide the sharper focus, the detail, the depth of knowledge that you didn't have before, generating an overall superior picture. Enjoy the view.

*—Rob Mains is an author of Baseball Prospectus.*

# Statistical Introduction

Sports are, fundamentally, a blend of athletic endeavor and storytelling. Baseball, like any other sport, tells its stories in so many ways: in the arc of a game from the stands or a season from the box scores, in photos, or even in numbers. At Baseball Prospectus, we understand that statistics don't replace observation or any of baseball's stories, but complement everything else that makes the game so much fun.

What stats help us with is with patterns and precision, variance and value. This book can help you learn things you may not see from watching a game or hundred, whether it's the path of a career over time or the breadth of the entire MLB. We'd also never ask you to choose between our numbers and the experience of viewing a game from the cheap seats or the comfort of your home; our publication combines running the numbers with observations and wisdom from some of the brightest minds we can find. But if you *do* want to learn more about the numbers beyond what's on the backs of player jerseys, let us help explain.

## Offense

At the end of this past year, we've revised our methodology for determining batting value. Long-time readers of Baseball Prospectus will notice that we've retired True Average in favor of a new metric: Deserved Runs Created Plus (DRC+). Developed by Jonathan Judge and our stats team, this statistic measures everything a player does at the plate–reaching base, hitting for power, making outs, and moving runners over–and puts it on a scale where 100 equals league-average performance. A DRC+ of 150 is terrific, a DRC+ of 100 is average, and a DRC+ of 75 means you better be an excellent defender.

DRC+ also does a better job than any of our previous metrics in taking contextual factors into account. The model adjusts for how the park affects performance, but also for things like the talent of the opposing pitcher, value of different types of batted-ball events, league, temperature, and other factors. It's able to describe a player's expected offensive contribution than any other statistic we've found over the years, and also does a better job of predicting future performance as well.

The other aspect of run-scoring is baserunning, which we quantify using Baserunning Runs. BRR not only records the value of stolen bases (or getting caught in the act), but also accounts for a runner's ability to go first to third on a single or advance on a fly ball.

## Defense

Where offensive value is *relatively* easy to identify and understand, defensive value is ... not. Over the past dozen years, the sabermetric community has focused mostly on stats based on zone data: a real-live human person records the type of batted ball and estimated landing location, and models are created that give expected outs. From there, you can compare fielders' actual outs to those expected ones. Simple, right?

Unfortunately, zone data has two major issues. First, zone data is recorded by commercial data providers who keep the raw data private unless you pay for it. (All the statistics we build in this book and on our website use public data as inputs.) That hurts our ability to test assumptions or duplicate results. Second, over the years it has become apparent that there's quite a bit of "noise" in zone-based fielding analysis. Sometimes the conclusions drawn from zone data don't hold up to scrutiny, and sometimes the different data provided by different providers don't look anything alike, giving wildly different results. Sometimes the hard-working professional stringers or scorers might unknowingly inflict unconscious bias into the mix: for example good fielders will often be credited with more expected outs despite the data, and ballparks with high press boxes tend to score more line drives than ones with a lower press box.

Enter our Fielding Runs Above Average (FRAA). For most positions, FRAA is built from play-by-play data, which allows us to avoid the subjectivity found in many other fielding metrics. The idea is this: count how many fielding plays are made by a given player and compare that to expected plays for an average fielder at their position (based on pitcher ground-ball tendencies and batter handedness). Then we adjust for park and base-out situations.

When it comes to catchers, our methodology is a little different thanks to the laundry list of responsibilities they're tasked with beyond just, well, catching and throwing the ball. By now you've probably heard about "framing" or the art of making umpires more likely to call balls outside the strike zone for strikes. To put this into one tidy number, we incorporate pitch tracking data (for the years it exists) and adjust for important factors like pitcher, umpire, batter, and home-field advantage using a mixed-model approach. This grants us a number for how many strikes the catcher is personally adding to (or subtracting from) his pitchers' performance ... which we then convert to runs added or lost using linear weights.

Framing is one of the biggest parts of determining catcher value, but we also take into account blocking balls from going past, whether a scorer deems it a passed ball or a wild pitch. We use a similar approach–one that really benefits from the pitch tracking data that tells us what ends up in the dirt and what doesn't. We also include a catcher's ability to prevent stolen bases and how well they field balls in play, and *finally* we come up with our FRAA for catchers.

## Pitching

Both pitching and fielding make up the half of baseball that isn't run scoring: run prevention. Separating pitching from fielding is a tough task, and most recent pitching analysis has branched off from Voros McCracken's famous (and controversial) statement, "There is little if any difference among major-league pitchers in their ability to prevent hits on balls hit in the field of play." The research of the analytic community has validated this to some extent, and there are a host of "defense-independent" pitching measures that have been developed to try and extricate the effect of the defense behind a hurler from the pitcher's work.

Our solution to this quandary is Deserved Run Average (DRA), our core pitching metric. DRA looks like earned run average (ERA), the tried-and-true pitching stat you've seen on every baseball broadcast or box score from the past century, but it's very different. To start, DRA takes an event-by-event look at what the pitchers does, and adjusts the value of that event based on different environmental factors like park, batter, catcher, umpire, base-out situation, run differential, inning, defense, home field advantage, pitcher role, and temperature. That mixed model gives us a pitcher's expected contribution, similar to what we do for our DRC+ model for hitters and FRAA model for catchers. (Oh, and we also consider the pitcher's effect on basestealing and on balls getting past the catcher.)

It's important to note that DRA is set to the scale of runs allowed per nine innings (RA9) instead of ERA, which makes DRA's scale slightly higher than ERA's. The reason for this is because ERA tends to overrate three types of pitchers:

1. Pitchers who play in parks where scorers hand out more errors. Official scorers differ significantly in the frequency at which they assign errors to fielders.
2. Ground-ball pitchers, because a substantial proportion of errors occur on grounders.
3. Pitchers who aren't very good. Better pitchers often allow fewer unearned runs than bad pitchers, because good pitchers tend to find ways to get out of jams.

Since the last time you picked up an edition of this book, we've also made a few minor changes to DRA to make it better. Recent research into "tunneling"–the act of throwing consecutive pitches that appear similar from a batter's point of view until after the swing decision point–data has given us a new contextual factor to account for in DRA: plate distance. This refers to the distance between successive pitches as they approach the plate, and while it has a smaller effect than factors like velocity or whiff rate, it still can help explain pitcher strikeout rate in our model.

## New Pitching Metrics for 2019

We're including a few "new" pitching metrics for 2019's suite of Baseball Prospectus publications, but you may be familiar with them if you've spent time scouring the internet for stats.

### Fastball Percentage

Our fastball percentage (FB%) statistic measures how frequently a pitcher throws a pitch classified as a "fastball," measured as a percentage of overall pitches thrown. We qualify three types of fastballs:

1. The traditional four-seam fastball;
2. The two-seam fastball or sinker;
3. "Hard cutters," which are pitches that have the movement profile of a cut fastball and are used as the pitcher's primary offering or in place of a more traditional fastball.

For example, a pitcher with a FB% of 67 throws any combination of these three pitches about two-thirds of the time.

### Whiff Rate

Everybody loves a swing and a miss, and whiff rate (WHF) measures how frequently pitchers induce a swinging strike. To calculate WHF, we add up all the pitches thrown that ended with a swinging strike, then divide that number by a pitcher's total pitches thrown. Most often, high whiff rates correlate with high strikeout rates (and overall effective pitcher performance).

### Called Strike Probability

Called Strike Probability (CSP) is a number that represents the likelihood that all of a pitcher's pitches will be called a strike while controlling for location, pitcher and batter handedness, umpire and count. Here's how it works: on each pitch, our model determines how many times (out of 100) that a similar pitch was called for a strike given those factors mentioned above, and when normalized for each batter's strike zone. Then we average the CSP for all pitches thrown by a pitcher in a season, and that gives us the yearly CSP percentage you see in the stats boxes.

As you might imagine, pitchers with a higher CSP are more likely to work in the zone, where pitchers with a lower CSP are likely locating their pitches outside the normal strike zone, for better or for worse.

## Projections

Many of you aren't turning to this book just for a look at what a player has done, but for a look at what a player is going to do: the PECOTA projections. PECOTA, initially developed by Nate Silver (who has moved on to greater fame as a political analyst), consists of three parts:

1. Major-league equivalencies, which use minor-league statistics to project how a player will perform in the major leagues;
2. Baseline forecasts, which use weighted averages and regression to the mean to estimate a player's current true talent level; and
3. Aging curves, which uses the career paths of comparable players to estimate how a player's statistics are likely to change over time.

With all those important things covered, let's take a look at what's in the book this year.

## Team Prospectus

You bought this book to learn more about your favorite (or maybe least-favorite, who are we to judge?) team, so let's talk about them. After a thoughtful preview of the 2019 season, you'll be presented with our Team Prospectus. This outlines many of the key statistics for each team's 2018 season, as well as a very inviting stadium diagram.

First you'll find the Performance Graphs page. The first is the 2018 Hit List Ranking. This shows our Hit List Rank for the team on each day of the 2018 season and is intended to give you a picture of the ups and downs of the team's season, including their highest and lowest ranks of the year. Hit List Rank measures overall team performance and drives the Hit List Power Rankings at the baseballprospectus.com website.

The second graph is Committed Payroll and helps you see how the team's payroll has compared to the MLB and divisional average payrolls over time. Payroll figures are currents as of January 1, 2019; with so many free agents still unsigned as of this writing, the final 2018 figure will likely be significantly different for many teams. (In the meantime, you can always find the most current data at Baseball Prospectus' Cot's Baseball Contracts page.)

# Colorado Rockies 2019

The third graph is Farm System Ranking and displays how the Baseball Prospectus prospect team has ranked the organization's farm system since 2007. It also indicates the highest and lowest ranks that the farm system achieved over that time.

We start the Team Performance page with the squad's unadjusted and third-order 2018 win-loss records, presented in divisional context. We then list the three highest performing hitters and pitchers by WARP for 2018. Beneath that are a host of other team statistics. **Pythag** presents an adjusted 2018 winning percentage, calculated by taking runs scored per game (**RS/G**) and runs allowed per game (**RA/G**) for the team, and running them through a version of Bill James' Pythagorean formula that was refined and improved by David Smyth and Brandon Heipp. (The formula is called "Pythagenpat," which is equally fun to type and to say.)

Next up is **DRC+**, described earlier, to indicate the overall hitting ability of the team either above or below league-average. Run prevention on the pitching side is covered by **DRA** (also mentioned earlier) and another metric: Fielding Independent Pitching (**FIP**), which calculates another ERA-like statistic based on strikeouts, walks, and home runs recorded. Defensive Efficiency Rating (**DER**) tells us the percentage of balls in play turned into outs for the team, and is a quick fielding shorthand that rounds out run prevention.

After that, we have several measures related to roster composition, as opposed to on-field performance. **B-Age** and **P-Age** tell us the average age of a team's batters and pitchers, respectively. **Salary** is the combined team payroll for all on-field players, and Doug Pappas' Marginal Dollars per Marginal Win (**M$/MW**) tells us how much money a team spent to earn production above replacement level.

Ending this batch of statistics is the number of disabled list days a team had over the season (**DL Days**) and the amount of salary paid to players on the disabled list (**$ on DL**); this final number is expressed as a percentage of total payroll.

Next to each of these stats, we've listed each team's MLB rank in that category from 1st to 30th. In this, 1st always indicates a positive outcome and 30th a negative outcome, except in the case of salary–1st is highest.

The Team Projections page is intended to convey the team's operational capacity entering the 2019 season. We start with the team's PECOTA projected record for 2019, again in divisional context. The **+/-** column indicates how many more or less wins the team is projected to get than they got in 2018. We then list the three highest projected hitters and pitchers by WARP for 2018. A brief farm system summary follows, with the team's top prospect and number of BP Top 101 Prospects. Finally, we list the key new players and departed players, along with their 2019 projected WARP.

## Alex Bregman  3B

Born: 03/30/94   Age: 25   Bats: R   Throws: R
Height: 6'0"   Weight: 180   Origin: Round 1, 2015 Draft (#2 overall)

| YEAR | TEAM | LVL | AGE | PA | R | 2B | 3B | HR | RBI | BB | K | SB | CS | AVG/OBP/SLG |
|---|---|---|---|---|---|---|---|---|---|---|---|---|---|---|
| 2016 | CCH | AA | 22 | 285 | 54 | 16 | 2 | 14 | 46 | 42 | 26 | 5 | 3 | .297/.415/.559 |
| 2016 | FRE | AAA | 22 | 83 | 17 | 6 | 0 | 6 | 15 | 5 | 12 | 2 | 1 | .333/.373/.641 |
| 2016 | HOU | MLB | 22 | 217 | 31 | 13 | 3 | 8 | 34 | 15 | 52 | 2 | 0 | .264/.313/.478 |
| 2017 | HOU | MLB | 23 | 626 | 88 | 39 | 5 | 19 | 71 | 55 | 97 | 17 | 5 | .284/.352/.475 |
| 2018 | HOU | MLB | 24 | 705 | 105 | 51 | 1 | 31 | 103 | 96 | 85 | 10 | 4 | .286/.394/.532 |
| 2019 | HOU | MLB | 25 | 675 | 96 | 38 | 3 | 23 | 78 | 73 | 107 | 12 | 4 | .272/.359/.463 |

Breakout: 6%   Improve: 52%   Collapse: 5%   Attrition: 2%   MLB: 100%
Comparables: Anthony Rendon, David Wright, Pablo Sandoval

| YEAR | TEAM | LVL | AGE | PA | DRC+ | VORP | BABIP | BRR | FRAA | WARP |
|---|---|---|---|---|---|---|---|---|---|---|
| 2016 | CCH | AA | 22 | 285 | 172 | 38.9 | .286 | 1.6 | SS(51): -3.4, 3B(11): 1.4 | 2.7 |
| 2016 | FRE | AAA | 22 | 83 | 161 | 10.0 | .333 | -1.2 | SS(14): 2.1, LF(3): -0.1 | 0.8 |
| 2016 | HOU | MLB | 22 | 217 | 107 | 9.6 | .317 | 0.5 | 3B(40): 0.9, SS(6): -0.1 | 1.1 |
| 2017 | HOU | MLB | 23 | 626 | 114 | 34.7 | .311 | -1.5 | 3B(132): 8.7, SS(30): -2.9 | 3.9 |
| 2018 | HOU | MLB | 24 | 705 | 150 | 72.6 | .289 | -1.6 | 3B(136): 5.4, SS(28): -0.4 | 7.4 |
| 2019 | HOU | MLB | 25 | 675 | 125 | 37.3 | .295 | 0.0 | 3B 7, SS 0 | 4.6 |

After the projections page, we share a few items about the team's home ballpark. There's the aforementioned diagram of the park's dimensions (including distances to the outfield wall), a few important biographical facts about the stadium, a graphic showing the height of the wall from the left-field pole to the right-field pole, and a table showing three-year park factors for the stadium. The park factors are displayed as indexes where 100 is average, 110 means that the park inflates the statistic in question by 10 percent, and 90 means that the park deflates the statistic in question by 10 percent.

Following the ballpark page, we have a **Personnel** section that lists many of the important decision-makers and upper-level field and operations staff members for the franchise, as well as any former Baseball Prospectus staff members who are currently part of the organization.

## Position Players

After all that information and a thoughtful bylined essay covering each team, we present our player comments. Each player is listed with the major-league team who employed him as of early January 2019. If a player changed teams after that point via free agency, trade, or any other method, you'll be able to find them in the book for their previous squad.

First, we cover biographical information (age is as of June 30, 2019) before moving onto the stats themselves. Our statistic columns include standard identifying information like **YEAR**, **TEAM**, **LVL** (level of affiliated play) and **AGE** before getting into the numbers. Next, we provide raw, unstranslated numbers like you might find on the back of your dad's baseball cards: **PA** (plate appearances), **R** (runs), **2B** (doubles), **3B** (triples), **HR** (home runs), **RBI** (runs batted in), **BB** (walks), **K** (strikeouts), **SB** (stolen bases) and **CS** (caught stealing). Then we have unadjusted "slash" statistics: **AVG** (batting average), **OBP** (on-base percentage) and **SLG** (slugging percentage).

Just below the stats box is **PECOTA** data, which is discussed further in a following section. After that, it's on to a pithy and always-informative comment written by a member of the Baseball Prospectus staff, before we cover more stats.

The second text box repeats YEAR, TEAM, LVL, AGE, and PA, then moves on to **DRC+** (Deserved Runs Created Plus), which we described earlier as total offensive expected contribution compared to the league average. Next, one of our oldest active metrics, **VORP** (Value Over Replacement Player), considers offensive production, position and plate appearances. In essence, it is the number of runs contributed beyond what a replacement-level player at the same position would contribute if given the same percentage of team plate appearances. VORP does not consider the quality of a player's defense.

**BABIP** (batting average on balls in play) tells us how often a ball in play fell for a hit, and can help us identify whether a batter may have been lucky or not ... but note that high BABIPs also tend to follow the great hitters of our time, as well as speedy singles hitters who put the ball on the ground.

The next item is **BRR** (Baserunning Runs), which covers all of a player's baserunning accomplishments which includes (but isn't limited to) swiped bags and failed attempts. Next is **FRAA** (Fielding Runs Above Average), which also includes the number of games previously played at each position noted in parentheses. Multi-position players have only their two most frequent positions listed here, but their total FRAA number reflects all positions played.

Our last column here is **WARP** (Wins Above Replacement Player). WARP estimates the total value of a player, which means for hitters it takes into account hitting runs above average (calculated using the DRC+ model), BRR and FRAA. Then, it makes an adjustment for positions played and gives the player a credit for plate appearances based upon the difference between "replacement level"¬–which is derived from the quality of players added to a team's roster after the start of the season¬–and the league average.

## Catchers

Catchers are a special breed, and thus they have earned their own separate box which displays some of the defensive metrics that we've built just for them. As an example, let's check out J.T. Realmuto.

| YEAR | TEAM | P. COUNT | FRM RUNS | BLK RUNS | THRW RUNS | TOT RUNS |
|---|---|---|---|---|---|---|
| 2016 | MIA | 18935 | -8.5 | 1.8 | 2.1 | -5.6 |
| 2017 | MIA | 18959 | 5.3 | 1.7 | 1.0 | 9.1 |
| 2018 | MIA | 16399 | -0.4 | 0.9 | 0.1 | 0.4 |
| 2019 | PHI | 18448 | -1.4 | 1.5 | 0.7 | 0.8 |

The **YEAR** and **TEAM** columns match what you'd find in the other stat box. **P. COUNT** indicates the number of pitches thrown while the catcher was behind the plate, including swinging strikes, fouls, and balls in play. **FRM RUNS** is the total run value the catcher provided (or cost) his team by influencing the umpire to call strikes where other catchers did not. **BLK RUNS** expresses the total run value above or below average for the catcher's ability to prevent wild pitches and passed balls. **THRW RUNS** is calculated using a similar model as the previous two statistics, and it measures a catcher's ability to throw out basestealers but also to dissuade them from testing his arm in the first place. It takes into account factors like the pitcher (including his delivery and pickoff move) and baserunner (who could be as fast as Billy Hamilton or as slow as Yonder Alonso). **TOT RUNS** is the sum of all of the previous three statistics.

## Pitchers

Let's give our pitchers a turn, using 2018 NL Cy Young winner Jacob deGrom as our example. Take a look at his first stat block: the first line and the **YEAR**, **TEAM**, **LVL** and **AGE** columns are the same as in the position player example earlier.

Here too, we have a series of columns that display raw, unadjusted statistics compiled by the pitcher over the course of a season: **W** (wins), **L** (losses), **SV** (saves), **G** (games pitched), **GS** (games started), **IP** (innings pitched), **H** (hits allowed) and **HR** (home runs allowed). Next we have two statistics that are rates: **BB/9** (walks per nine innings) and **K/9** (strikeouts per nine innings), before returning to the unadjusted **K** (strikeouts).

Next up is **GB%** (ground ball percentage), which is the percentage of all batted balls that were hit in the ground, including both outs and hits. Remember, this is based on observational data and subject to human error, so please approach this with a healthy dose of skepticism.

**BABIP** (batting average on balls in play) is calculated using the same methodology as it is for position players, but it often tells us more about a pitcher than it does a hitter. With pitchers, a high BABIP is often due to poor defense or bad luck, and can often be an indicator of potential rebound, and a low BABIP may be cause to expect performance regression. (A typical league-average BABIP is close to .290-.300.)

After a witty 150ish words on the player like only Baseball Prospectus's staff can provide, it's on to that second stat block, which repeats the YEAR, TEAM, LVL, and AGE columns. The metrics **WHIP** (walks plus hits per inning pitched) and **ERA**

Colorado Rockies 2019

(earned run average) are old standbys: WHIP measures walks and hits allowed on a per-inning basis, while ERA measures earned runs on a nine-inning basis. Neither of these stats are translated or adjusted.

**DRA** (Deserved Run Average) was described at length earlier, and measures how many runs the pitcher "deserved" to allow per nine innings. Please note that since we lack all the data points that would make for a "real" DRA for minor-league events, the DRA displayed for minor league partial-seasons is based off of different data. (That data is a modified version of our cFIP metric, which you can find more information about on our website.)

## Jacob deGrom   RHP
Born: 06/19/88   Age: 31   Bats: L   Throws: R
Height: 6'4"   Weight: 180   Origin: Round 9, 2010 Draft (#272 overall)

| YEAR | TEAM | LVL | AGE | W | L | SV | G | GS | IP | H | HR | BB/9 | K/9 | K | GB% | BABIP |
|---|---|---|---|---|---|---|---|---|---|---|---|---|---|---|---|---|
| 2016 | NYN | MLB | 28 | 7 | 8 | 0 | 24 | 24 | 148 | 142 | 15 | 2.2 | 8.7 | 143 | 47% | .312 |
| 2017 | NYN | MLB | 29 | 15 | 10 | 0 | 31 | 31 | 201[1] | 180 | 28 | 2.6 | 10.7 | 239 | 48% | .305 |
| 2018 | NYN | MLB | 30 | 10 | 9 | 0 | 32 | 32 | 217 | 152 | 10 | 1.9 | 11.2 | 269 | 48% | .281 |
| 2019 | NYN | MLB | 31 | 13 | 9 | 0 | 31 | 31 | 186 | 145 | 18 | 2.3 | 10.7 | 221 | 46% | .286 |

Breakout: 8%   Improve: 29%   Collapse: 28%   Attrition: 6%   MLB: 85%
Comparables: Erik Bedard, A.J. Burnett, CC Sabathia

| YEAR | TEAM | LVL | AGE | WHIP | ERA | DRA | WARP | MPH | FB% | WHF | CSP |
|---|---|---|---|---|---|---|---|---|---|---|---|
| 2016 | NYN | MLB | 28 | 1.20 | 3.04 | 3.30 | 3.5 | 96.3 | 59.6 | 12.1 | 47.2 |
| 2017 | NYN | MLB | 29 | 1.19 | 3.53 | 3.02 | 5.7 | 97.2 | 55.5 | 14.5 | 49.5 |
| 2018 | NYN | MLB | 30 | 0.91 | 1.70 | 2.09 | 8.0 | 98.2 | 52.1 | 16.3 | 48.4 |
| 2019 | NYN | MLB | 31 | 1.02 | 2.91 | 3.23 | 3.9 | 96.6 | 54.5 | 14.8 | 48.2 |

Just like with hitters, **WARP** (Wins Above Replacement Player) is a total value metric that puts pitchers of all stripes on the same scale as position players. We use DRA as the primary input for our calculation of WARP. You might notice that relief pitchers (due to their limited innings) may have a lower WARP than you were expecting or than you might see in other WARP-like metrics. WARP does not take leverage into account, just the actions a pitcher performs and the expected value of those actions ... which ends up judging high-leverage relief pitchers differently than you might imagine given their prestige and market value.

**MPH** gives you the pitcher's 95th percentile velocity for the noted season, in order to give you an idea of what the *peak* fastball velocity a pitcher possesses. Since this comes from our pitch tracking data, it is not publicly available for minor-league pitchers.

Finally, we display the three new pitching metrics we described earlier. **FB%** (fastball percentage) gives you the percentage of fastballs thrown out of all pitches. **WhiffRt** (whiff rate) tells you the percentage of swinging strikes induced out of all pitches. **CS Prob** (called strike probability) expresses the likelihood of all pitches thrown to result in a called strike, after controlling for factors like handedness, umpire, pitch type, count, and location.

## PECOTA

All players have PECOTA projections for 2019, as well as a set of other numbers that describe the performance of comparable players according to PECOTA. All projections for 2019 are for the player at the date we went to press in early January and are projected into the league and park context as indicated by the team abbreviation. All PECOTA projected statistics represent a player's projected major-league performance.

The numbers beneath the player's stats–Breakout, Improve, Collapse, Attrition–are part and parcel of the PECOTA projections. They estimate the likelihood of changes in performance relative to the player's previously-established level of production, based on the performance of comparable players:

**Breakout Rate** is the percent change that a player's production will improve by at least 20 percent relative to the weighted average of his performance over his most recent seasons.

**Improve Rate** is the percent chance that a player's production will improve at all relative to his baseline performance. A player who is expected to perform just the same as he has in the recent past will have an Improve Rate of 50 percent.

**Collapse Rate** is the percent chance that a position player's production will decline by at least 25 percent relative to his baseline performance.

**Attrition Rate** operates on playing time rather than performance. Specifically, it measures the likelihood that a player's playing time will decrease by at least 50 percent relative to his established level.

Breakout Rate and Collapse Rate can sometimes be counterintuitive for players who have already experienced a radical change in performance level. It's also worth noting that the projected decline in a player's rate performances might not be indicative of an expected decline in underlying ability or skill, but could just be an anticipated correction following a breakout season.

MLB% is the percentage of similar players who played in the major leagues in their relevant season.

The final pieces of information are the player's three highest-scoring comparable players as determined by PECOTA. All comparables represent a snapshot of how the listed player was performing at the same age as the current player, so if a 23-year-old pitcher is compared to Bartolo Colon, he's actually being compared to a 23-year-old Colon, not the version that pitched for the Rangers in 2018, nor to Colon's career as a whole.

A few points about pitcher projections. First, we aren't yet projecting peak velocity, so that column will be blank in the PECOTA lines. Second, projecting DRA is trickier than evaluating past performance, because it is unclear how deserving each pitcher will be of his anticipated outcomes. However, we know that another DRA-related statistic–contextual FIP or cFIP–estimates future run scoring very well. So for PECOTA, the projected DRA figures you see are based on the past cFIPs generated by the pitcher and comparable players over time, along with the other factors described above.

## Lineouts

In each chapter's Lineouts section, you'll find abbreviated text comments, as well as most of same information you'd find in our full player comments. We limit the stats boxes in this section to only including the 2018 information for each player.

## Exclusive Player Visualizations

In our constant battle to provide you with new and interesting baseball content you can't find anywhere else, we've added a trio of data visualizations to each hitter's entry in these books and a pair of visualizations for each pitcher.

For hitters, you'll find three new infographics. The first is each player's **Batted Ball Distribution**, which displays the five major sections of the field: LF (left), LCF (left center), CF (center), RCF (right center), and RF (right). The percentage indicated tells us what percentage of batted balls from that hitter fell within that part of the field during the 2018 season. We've also included the hitter's slugging percentage on balls in play (also called **SLGCON**) for that part of the field.

You'll also see two heatmaps: **Strike Zone vs LHP** and **Strike Zone vs RHP**. These heat maps represent a view of the strike zone from behind the catcher. Areas where there is a darker coloration represent the places where a higher percentage of pitches resulted in hits. In other words, the heatmap represents a hitter's "sweet spots" for getting hits against either left-handed or right-handed pitchers, depending on the image.

Pitchers get two images that help explain what their pitches look like from a hitter's perspective: **Pitch Shape vs LHH** and **Pitch Shape vs RHH**. These images show you the shape and the "tunneling" effect of each pitcher's offerings from the batter's perspective. For each type of pitch that a pitcher throws (represented by an indicator shape), there's a set of dots indicating the flight path, where each dot represents a 0.01-second interval. This maps the average trajectory and speed of an offering, ending where the ball crosses the plate. The solid black box represents the regular strike zone, while the gray contour lines indicate the range of locations that a pitcher typically works in.

Below the image, we provide a bit more detailed information about each pitcher's average offering in the **Pitch Types** box. Here, we also list each of the pitcher's major offerings under the **Type** column.

- **Fastballs** (which usually refers to the four-seam variation)
- **Sinkers** and/or two-seam fastballs
- **Cutters** (which could include "hard" cutters like cut fastballs and "soft" cutters that resemble hard sliders)
- **Changeups** (not including most splitters)
- **Splitters** (split-fingered pitches, forkballs, and some split-changes)
- **Sliders** and/or slurves
- **Curveballs** (including spike-curveballs and knuckle-curveballs, as well as some slurvy curves)
- **Slow curveballs** and/or eephus pitches
- **Knuckleballs**
- **Screwballs**

The **Freq** column indicates the percentage of overall pitches that fall into each of those type categories; if a pitcher has a 16.55% score for changeups, then that's the percent of all pitches that he throws as changeups. **Velo** is exactly what you think it is: the average miles per hour for each pitch type. **H Mov** is the number of inches of horizontal movement on the average pitch of that type, while **V Mov** is the number of inches of vertical movement on the average pitch of that type. (At Baseball Prospectus, we measure this over the long flight of the ball and include gravity into the V Mov number in order to give you the most realistic representation of what the pitch *actually* does.)

If you're wondering about the second number in brackets, that's the index for that velocity or movement compared to the league average. Like DRC+, a score of 100 means that the speed or movement is about the same as league average, while a higher score means that there's higher velocity or movement than the league average. Numbers below 100 indicate less velocity or movement than the league average.

# Part 1: Team Analysis

# Table for Two: Previewing the 2019 Colorado Rockies

Jen Mac Ramos and Jeffrey Paternostro

**How did the team approach the offseason, and did they do well given their aims?**

**JEFFREY PATERNOSTRO:** I've long stated that I don't fully comprehend how the Rockies work. This isn't due to a sense of naive wonderment, as with the Insane Clown Posse w/r/t magnets, but more a pervasive, general befuddlement. Occasionally bemusement, if I'm honest. I'm not suggesting they're even wrong, man, just confusing. However, I can't deny that it's worked recently, and as we head into the 2019 campaign, even I can't quibble with extending Nolan Arenado, putting Daniel Murphy at elevation with big outfield gaps to shoot for, or doing a like-for-like swap with DJ LeMahieu and Garrett Hampson.

Ideally, you would have preferred Colorado to bring in one or two more proven pen options—and hey, there are still a few out there here in March—but they did a nice job consolidating and improving their 2018 playoff team. Now, it's still the Rockies, so they are also talking about playing Ian Desmond in center field in 2019. Baby steps towards sensibleness though.

**JEN MAC RAMOS:** I also will never understand how the Rockies work. Not because their moves seem like it'll be bad, but more because it seems so outlandish that it could never work, and yet there's usually a more than 50 percent chance that it does. They certainly made big moves as far as extending Arenado goes and on paper, the Daniel Murphy signing seems smart. But we'll wait and see how that goes with the state of the rest of the lineup. I think there's still some room for improvement as far as strengthening their rotation and bullpen goes, but the idea of pitching at Coors Field is never appealing for anyone.

I refuse to talk about Ian Desmond playing center field, in 2019 or otherwise.

**Who is your team's breakout player for 2019?**

**JEFFREY:** For the third straight year I am betting on a breakout season from David Dahl. He finally got healthy at the end of 2018, and the Rockies seem actually willing this go round to give him a full-time outfield job—although there is always time enough at last for another one-year CarGo deal. Dahl can still get a little pull-happy at times, but statistically speaking it's more "above-average pullside" than the "YOLO grip it 'n' rip it" strategy he employed a lot of the time in the minors. He's always been a good fit for Coors Field—sure, that applies to anyone who makes enough contact and has plus raw power—and is a better fit for center than, well, Ian Desmond.

This is still true even after his litany of injuries has sapped some of his explosiveness and tempered the speed part of his power/speed combo. The power is still there, though, and he could bop 40 home runs with a full season of at-bats. It took me some time to come around on Dahl the prospect, but I'm still a believer in big things for Dahl the major leaguer. And while it feels like he should be older than this, he'll turn just 25 on Opening Day. He just needs to stay healthy, which is also something I'm writing for the third straight year

**JEN:** My guess this year is that'll be Garrett Hampson. He's a solid, above-average middle infielder who could be DJ LeMahieu lite in his (most likely) first full season in the big leagues. He's not necessarily Mike Trout at the plate, but more of a contact hitter than anything. He's capable of ground-ball base hits—and a lot of them, natch—and occasionally balls doinking in for hits in outfield gaps. His ability to steal bases hints at him as a potential leadoff hitter throughout the season.

He shows extremely good range at second base, after having shifted to the position upon entering professional baseball (he was a shortstop at Long Beach State), and the way he fields the ball to making the throws looks so seamless. Provided that the Rockies don't choose to have someone else start at second base or, for whatever reason, they decide to throw Desmond at second, Hampson looks like the most obvious choice to start.

**JEFFREY:** I am pretty sure we have quorum for the Garrett Hampson Appreciation Society just in this preview.

**What part of the team can you simply not go along with PECOTA on?**

**JEN:** There's actually not much I disagree with PECOTA about when it comes to the Rockies. The thing that I've always noticed with the Rockies and projections, though, is that if it's a strong team (i.e. the 2017 and 2018 teams), the Rockies find a way to overperform and exceed expectations. They might not end up in the World Series, but it's hard to count them out of the postseason race.

Potentially undervaluing the team has its upsides. When you think about it, there's both a high and a low bar for them—a high bar for them to reach when it comes to overall team success, and a low bar for roster moves that can be puzzling. The team's potential can match the PECOTA projections, but it's hard to say if the Rockies can manage to create a sustainable roster throughout the whole season. Between injury-prone players and a sometimes shaky pitching staff, you can't really go on the higher end of the projections because it can be too risky.

**JEFFREY:** PECOTA and I both see the Rockies as a clear Wild Card contender with an outside punt at the NL West crown. Why I might consider them a wild card *favorite*, while the algorithm sees them as part of a mass of 85ish-win teams might come down to Kyle Freeland. Look supercomputer, I don't know exactly how Freeland has done it either. It feels like 2017 was closer to the version of the guy I saw as a prospect. Maybe a little bit better than I expected, but in that nebulous 3/4 starter zone.

It's a profile that absolutely shouldn't work toeing the mound half the time at elevation, but there's reasons to believe it's sustainable. Sometimes the multiple 55-pitches dudes play up as they learn to mix their stuff. And even if Freeland slides back towards the 2017 version, that's a sight better than PECOTA has him projected, and a big reason the Rockies might end up closer to 90 wins than 85.

**How will this team end up, and what kind of path will they take to get there?**

**JEFFREY:** While there has been plenty of copy already filed about how competitive the NL East and Central will be in 2019, the West may be sneaky tough as well. Even after signing Machado, you'd suspect the Padres are still a year away, but I've thought that about the Braves and Brewers in recent years. The perennial favorites in Chavez Ravine has a staff ace who is uncomfortable playing catch, and the rest of their rotation is about as durable as your grandmother's stemware. The Giants may or may not have signed Bryce Harper by the time you read this, and even without Paul Goldschmidt the Diamondbacks will at least qualify as "frisky." It's not exactly wide open, but it's very winnable.

The Rockies have the depth internally to fill in around the margins too. If Garrett Hampson struggles in his first extended look in the majors—although both Jen and I doubt that—top prospect Brendan Rodgers will be ready to step in. They have Raimel Tapia lurking as a fourth outfielder and arms like Peter Lambert and Yency Almonte able to contribute in a swiss army arm type role in case of injury or underperformance.

The field staff been particularly good with pitcher usage and while I can quibble more broadly about how they've handled young position prospects—we have Pat Valaika projected for almost as many PA as Garrett Hampson or Ryan McMahon—they have an experienced roster that should be in and around the playoff picture all season. Since it's *de rigueur* to end this with a record prediction, I'll go with 88 wins and the first wild card with the impending donnybrooks in the other National League divisions opening a lane for the Rockies to cruise through.

**JEN:** At best, this Rockies team can end up walking away with a Wild Card spot. The NL West has been the wild west the last few seasons because you never really knew which of the top teams would end up going to the postseason, but with both the Giants and the Diamondbacks going through some kind of rebuilding process, the Rockies have a clearer path to one of the top two spots in the division. The Padres can sneak up on them, though, because there's really no telling how their season will play out after signing Manny Machado.

It won't be an easy process for the Rockies, though. The Dodgers are still a very good team and they're not going to relinquish being the reigning NL champs if they can help it. But this Rockies team can offset any pitching woes they have with a stronger offense, though that can only be a temporary fix. Like Jeff said, the Rockies have internal options to fill in the margins, but I worry that might not be enough for them. My guess is that if the Rockies find themselves in a position where they can trade for a reliable ace or a lights out reliever at the deadline, they'll go for it and that might be the key for them to make it back into the postseason.

# Performance Graphs

### *2018 Hit List Ranking*

### **Committed Payroll (in millions)**

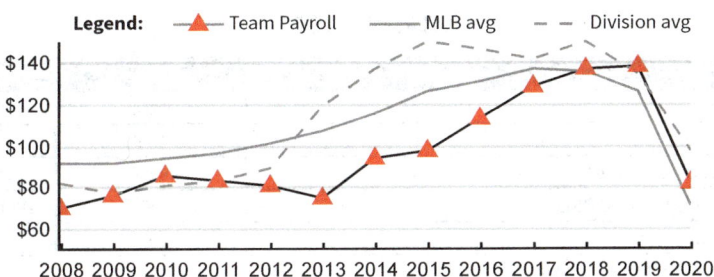

### **Farm System Ranking**

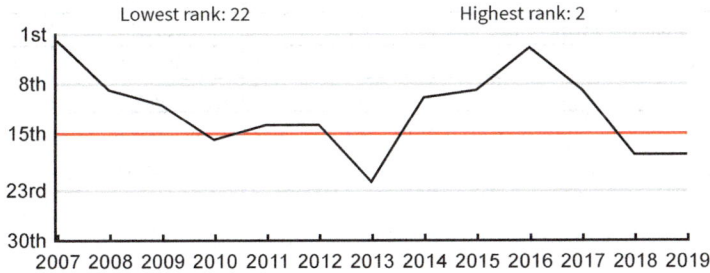

# 2018 Team Performance

## ACTUAL STANDINGS

| Team | W | L | Pct |
|---|---|---|---|
| LAN | 92 | 71 | .564 |
| **COL** | **91** | **72** | **.558** |
| ARI | 82 | 80 | .506 |
| SFN | 73 | 89 | .450 |
| SDN | 66 | 96 | .407 |

## THIRD-ORDER STANDINGS

| Team | W | L | Pct |
|---|---|---|---|
| LAN | 105 | 58 | .644 |
| **COL** | **88** | **75** | **.539** |
| ARI | 87 | 75 | .537 |
| SFN | 71 | 91 | .438 |
| SDN | 66 | 96 | .407 |

## TOP HITTERS

| Player | WARP |
|---|---|
| Nolan Arenado | 6.2 |
| Trevor Story | 5 |
| Mike Tauchman | 4.8 |

## TOP PITCHERS

| Player | WARP |
|---|---|
| German Marquez | 4.7 |
| Kyle Freeland | 3.3 |
| Jeff Hoffman | 1.7 |

## VITAL STATISTICS

| Statistic Name | Value | Rank |
|---|---|---|
| Pythagenpat | .522 | 14th |
| Runs Scored per Game | 4.79 | 7th |
| Runs Allowed per Game | 4.57 | 20th |
| Deserved Runs Created Plus | 96 | 16th |
| Deserved Run Average | 4.48 | 18th |
| Fielding Independent Pitching | 4.02 | 14th |
| Defensive Efficiency Rating | .700 | 22nd |
| Batter Age | 28.7 | 23rd |
| Pitcher Age | 27.2 | 7th |
| Salary | $137.0M | 14th |
| Marginal $ per Marginal Win | $2.9M | 22nd |
| Disabled List Days | $891.0M | 7th |
| $ on DL | 7% | 1st |

# 2019 Team Projections

## PROJECTED STANDINGS

| Team | W | L | Pct | +/- |
|---|---|---|---|---|
| LAN | 93 | 69 | .574 | +1 |
| **COL** | **84** | **78** | **.518** | **-7** |
| ARI | 81 | 81 | .500 | -1 |
| SDN | 79 | 83 | .487 | +13 |
| SFN | 73 | 89 | .450 | 0 |

## TOP PROJECTED HITTERS

| Player | WARP |
|---|---|
| Nolan Arenado | 5.0 |
| Charlie Blackmon | 4.1 |
| Daniel Murphy | 4.0 |

## TOP PROJECTED PITCHERS

| Player | WARP |
|---|---|
| German Marquez | 3.2 |
| Jon Gray | 2.4 |
| Kyle Freeland | 1.5 |

## FARM SYSTEM REPORT

| Top Prospect | Number of Top 101 Prospects |
|---|---|
| Brendan Rodgers, #22 | 2 |

## KEY DEDUCTIONS

| Player | WARP |
|---|---|
| DJ LeMahieu | 2.9 |
| Gerardo Parra | 0.8 |
| Adam Ottavino | 0.7 |

## KEY ADDITIONS

| Player | WARP |
|---|---|
| Daniel Murphy | 4.0 |
| Mark Reynolds | 0.3 |

# Team Personnel

**General Manager**
Jeff Bridich

**Assistant General Manager**
Zach Rosenthal

**Assistant General Manager - Player Personnel**
Jon Weil

**Senior Director, Player Development**
Zach Wilson

**Manager**
Bud Black

# Coors Field Stats

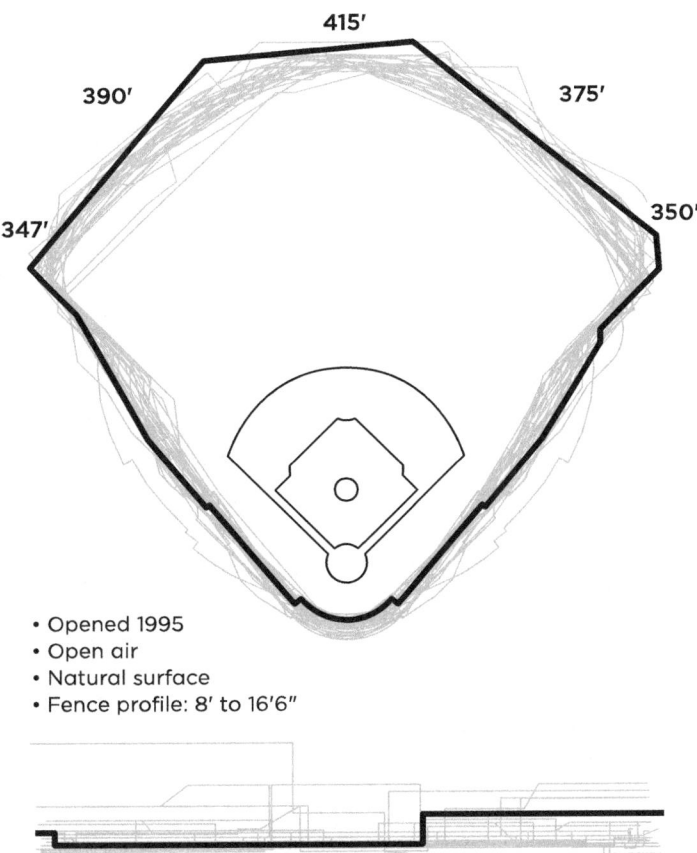

- Opened 1995
- Open air
- Natural surface
- Fence profile: 8' to 16'6"

## Three-Year Park Factors

| Runs | Runs/RH | Runs/LH | HR/RH | HR/LH |
|------|---------|---------|-------|-------|
| 112  | 113     | 110     | 110   | 109   |

# Rockies Team Analysis

The Rockies reached the playoffs in consecutive years for the first time in franchise history, have a young and self-developed starting rotation, boast arguably the best left side of the infield in baseball with Nolan Arenado and Trevor Story, and added a balls-in-play machine who should be perfect for Coors Field when they addressed their biggest need of the offseason with the signing of Daniel Murphy.

They've also won one playoff game in those two October appearances, have refused to either trade prospects for key upgrades or lean on positional prospects the way they have their young pitchers, hurled money at people named Ian Desmond, are a year away from possibly losing the best third baseman in the game as a free agent, and their big winter addition is an avatar for social division through the prism of baseball.

Whether you're an analyst or a fan, the side you take on the Rockies entering 2019 is not wrong. The Rockies are a team of opposites: one on the rise, whose time is almost up; playing with house money, but with twenty-five years of expectations heaped on them; and a group of lovable ragtag underdogs, and also…not so universally loveable. How this team looks at any moment depends entirely on the light. And yet there's one thing you can't say about this team that has been said about so many earlier iterations: that it's hopeless. The Dodgers still have their six-year run of division titles, and will be favored to make it seven, but the Rockies may have their best chance yet to overcome Los Angeles' baked-in advantages.

The Rockies' quarter-century existence has been all about overcoming everyone else's baked-in advantages, and it's possible that they have finally figured out the solution on the biggest one. The intense difference between playing in Colorado and playing everywhere else is something that no contemporary team has to deal with, with maybe the only comparison even approaching it being the Phillies, when they called Baker Bowl home. It's not just the ballpark, though, as I found last year when I wrote a piece for Rockies Magazine centered around asking players what people might not understand about Coors Life. The most interesting response belonged to Charlie Blackmon, who noted the physical toll of spending six months traveling in and out of Denver and constantly adjusting to life at altitude, namely fatigue, sleep issues, and dehydration.

# Colorado Rockies 2019

What Blackmon talked about is in addition to some things that get talked about often, namely when it comes to pitching. Catcher and wild card hero Tony Wolters brought up how pitches have a different shape to them in Denver, while erstwhile ace Jon Gray was open about the mental challenge of pitching in a huge park where lots of balls find grass but also plays like it has much shorter fences. No truism of baseball has held stronger than the suffocation of starting pitching in Coors, from Nied straight through Hampton and Neagle to Eddie Butler.

And now the Rockies are a pitching-first team that went 40-27 after last year's All-Star break, including 19-9 in September, to hold off the Dodgers and force a Game 163. Everything about the Rockies' position in the baseball universe says that should not be able to happen, yet it did.

It's not that the Rockies suddenly solved the issue of how to build a team that can succeed in Colorado. Instead, the unlikely success of Colorado's rotation was the culmination of long-term planning on multiple fronts, including having a farm system in which Double-A Hartford is the only affiliate that plays at an altitude of less than 2000 feet above sea level, with Triple-A Albuquerque clocking in 39 feet above Denver. The Rockies used seven starting pitchers in 2018. Tyler Anderson, Kyle Freeland, and Gray were Colorado's own first-round draft picks. Chad Bettis was a second-rounder. Antonio Senzatela signed with the Rockies as a 16-year-old out of Venezuela. German Marquez and Jeff Hoffman were acquired in trades as minor leaguers. Nearly all of them walked the same path up that metaphorical and very literal mountain.

It's not just the starting pitchers, though. From 2014-18, there were 25 different players who made Baseball Prospectus' annual top 10 lists of Rockies prospects. As of December, 21 remained in the organization. That includes every starter from last year other than Marquez, as well as Story, David Dahl, and Raimel Tapia. They also include Blackmon and Arenado, the Rockies' second-round picks in 2008 and 2009 who were well past prospect status by 2014 but clearly fit into the homegrown theme, not to mention the general manager, Jeff Bridich, who was promoted from farm director in 2014.

The strange thing about this is that the Rockies are more committed than any team since the reserve clause to winning with their own guys, yet they only really have been willing to stick with the young pitchers through their major league growing pains. Not so the position players. The Rockies played Ian Desmond at first base 138 times among his team-leading 160 appearances, not including starts at first base in all four of Colorado's playoff games, during which he went 2-for-17 with no extra-base hits, no walks, five strikeouts, and the flyout to center field that ended the season.

Desmond hit .236/.307/.422 for the season, and defied Rockies tradition by posting a higher slugging percentage on the road (.438) than at home (.404). His 22-homer campaign wasn't without highlights: a tiebreaking dinger off Sean

Doolittle in Washington in April, a walkoff two-run shot off Kirby Yates in August, another two-run blast off Joe Ross to put the Rockies ahead to stay in the win that clinched a playoff spot. Still, Desmond's 619-plate appearance season clocked in at 0.4 WARP, the same figure Garrett Hampson posted in 48 trips to the plate.

The Rockies gave a combined 1,865 plate appearances in 2018 to Desmond and veterans Carlos Gonzalez, Gerardo Parra, and Chris Iannetta, and a combined 373 trips to the plate for Ryan McMahon, Hampson, Tapia, and Tom Murphy. The team with the worst VORP among the 10 playoff lineups in 2018 went through the summer and added two position players, signing age-38 Matt Holliday as a free agent on July 29 and trading for age-34 Drew Butera on August 31. While other teams picked up bench bats like Justin Bour and Lucas Duda, the Rockies saw no need to upgrade their woeful offense.

The bullpen was even more stark in the Rockies' prioritization of form over payroll space. Bryan Shaw, given a three-year, $27 million deal before last season, stunk for the better part of five months and was relegated in September to four extremely low-leverage appearances. Jake McGee, with the same contract, made 11 appearances from August 26 through the end of the season, and was asked to protect a lead only once: September 25, when he came in with a seven-run cushion and gave up two runs to the Phillies in one-third of an inning. By the end of the season, Bud Black's most trusted setup men were Adam Ottavino, Scott Oberg, and July acquisition Seunghwan Oh.

The failure to either let young players play or trade for lineup help almost certainly cost the Rockies what could have been their first ever National League West title in 2018, but the steadfast refusal to part with prospects may be what sets up Colorado to win in 2019 and beyond.

The Rockies tied a record in 2018 with 163 games started by pitchers with 150 or fewer games of major league experience, a year after doing the same thing in all 162 of their games. Sticking with young pitchers through their ups and downs has brought the Rockies to a place where, for the first time ever, the starting rotation is their greatest strength. What if they'd done the same with the position players, though? Their rotation is so good and still so young, with nobody even set to reach free agency until Bettis does after the 2020 season. At the same time, Arenado hits free agency after 2019, which will be an inflection point for the organization whether the third baseman stays or goes.

The shame is that it shouldn't have to be. In a way the Rockies are a distillation of the current economic climate of baseball: half a roster of underpaid, cost-controlled talents, sharing a locker room with overpaid, free-agent veterans. There will always be the latter (and they deserve it, they were underpaid themselves) but it's particularly painful to consider the possibility of a team not being able to afford their franchise player with so much misspent salary on the books.

## Colorado Rockies 2019

But we are we are, which makes the 2019 so critical for the franchise. And the team approached it by making another veteran investment, though perhaps a more dramatic one than the Desmonds of the past, in three-time All-Star Daniel Murphy. In a way the acquisition is a culmination of everything Rockies, since he's as fractious as a player as the team itself. The team's new first baseman has made a career out of putting balls in play, and could easily be imagined following in the footsteps of Andres Galarraga, Michael Cuddyer, and Justin Morneau as late-career batting champions in Colorado. Then again, Murphy is entering his age 34 season, is coming off an injury-marred 2018 season, and has divided fanbases in multiple cities through his homophobic comments.

It's very easy to imagine Murphy being the story of the 2019 Colorado Rockies, and for that story to either end in triumph or shame. It's also very easy to imagine that story being the rise of Brendan Rodgers, or David Dahl, or the resurgence of Wade Davis. Or how German Marquez vanished as suddenly as he seemed to appear. As problematic as this team is, there are very few so interesting.

It's an exciting time to be a Rockies fan, a time when the second wild card was followed by getting to Game 163 and the NLDS, leading into a season with that whole young rotation hitting its stride, with an incredible left side of the infield, with a first baseman who fits exactly what the lineup needed, with a bunch of young players ready to show why Colorado was right not to trade them. The Rockies remain a fascinating, flawed franchise, but for perhaps the first time in a long time, it's a new flaw. And while the team may throw its money in the wrong direction sometimes, that's a much more interesting, and easily fixed, problem than watching flat curveballs get clubbed into the upper decks, year after year. It's by no means certain what fans will get with this team, but this may be the most exciting time for the Rockies since the initial joy of just having a major league team in Colorado.

—*Jesse Spector is a freelance baseball and hockey writer in New York, NY.*

# Part 2: Player Analysis

## Nolan Arenado  3B

Born: 04/16/91   Age: 28   Bats: R   Throws: R
Height: 6'2"   Weight: 205   Origin: Round 2, 2009 Draft (#59 overall)

| YEAR | TEAM | LVL | AGE | PA | R | 2B | 3B | HR | RBI | BB | K | SB | CS | AVG/OBP/SLG |
|---|---|---|---|---|---|---|---|---|---|---|---|---|---|---|
| 2016 | COL | MLB | 25 | 696 | 116 | 35 | 6 | 41 | 133 | 68 | 103 | 2 | 3 | .294/.362/.570 |
| 2017 | COL | MLB | 26 | 680 | 100 | 43 | 7 | 37 | 130 | 62 | 106 | 3 | 2 | .309/.373/.586 |
| 2018 | COL | MLB | 27 | 673 | 104 | 38 | 2 | 38 | 110 | 73 | 122 | 2 | 2 | .297/.374/.561 |
| 2019 | COL | MLB | 28 | 649 | 89 | 37 | 4 | 31 | 100 | 70 | 110 | 3 | 2 | .293/.373/.536 |

Breakout: 1%   Improve: 36%   Collapse: 12%   Attrition: 1%   MLB: 99%
Comparables: Ryan Zimmerman, Eric Chavez, George Brett

Arenado possesses one of the truly elite attack swings in baseball, his ferocious hacks sprung off a deep back-leg load with lightning-bolt hands guiding immense force. It is a swing that has now damaged baseballs in all directions of the atmospheric void in Denver for six seasons running, with the four most recent fusing to create a model of expert-level offensive consistency. And there's been plenty of elite defensive consistency, too. After a four-year run as one of the very best hot corner gloves in the world, the leather has held to very, very good over the last two. He'll have the opportunity to descend from the mile-high mountaintop and homestead in any of 29 other big-league valleys next winter coming off this, his age-28 season. When he does he'll probably be riding the wake of yet another brilliant effort and sitting on somewhere around 40 WARP for his career. Yet he'll inevitably stare down questions about sea-level adjusted production that'll cloud up the whole damn salary calculator, and that'll be a shame. That's next year, though. For now, we get another chance to admire an in-altitude, in-prime season of a player on a Hall-of-Fame track. And that's a fun thing to watch.

| YEAR | TEAM | LVL | AGE | PA | DRC+ | VORP | BABIP | BRR | FRAA | WARP |
|---|---|---|---|---|---|---|---|---|---|---|
| 2016 | COL | MLB | 25 | 696 | 128 | 52.5 | .293 | -0.9 | 3B(160): 23.0 | 7.1 |
| 2017 | COL | MLB | 26 | 680 | 136 | 63.0 | .320 | -0.5 | 3B(157): 5.0 | 6.0 |
| 2018 | COL | MLB | 27 | 673 | 138 | 47.5 | .314 | -2.9 | 3B(152): 9.1 | 6.2 |
| 2019 | COL | MLB | 28 | 649 | 134 | 42.8 | .315 | -1.2 | 3B 7 | 5.0 |

**Nolan Arenado, continued**

**Batted Ball Distribution**

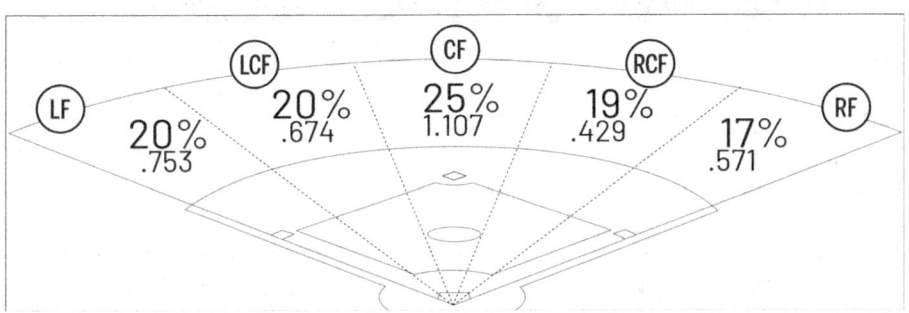

**Strike Zone vs LHP**     **Strike Zone vs RHP**

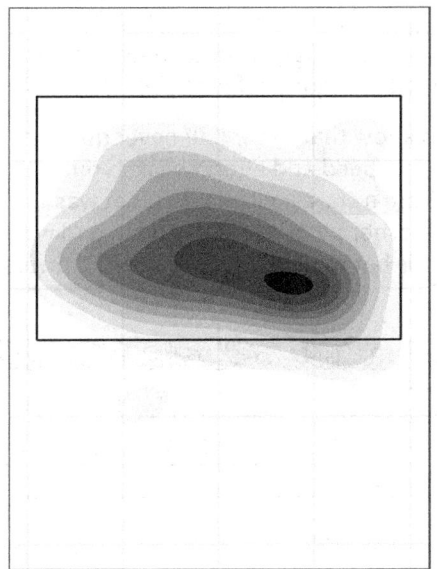 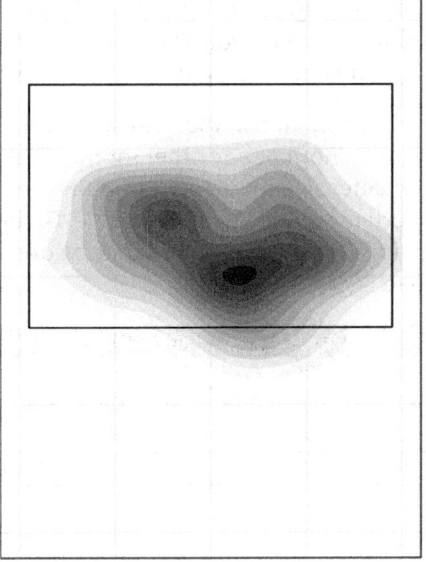

## Charlie Blackmon  CF

Born: 07/01/86  Age: 32  Bats: L  Throws: L
Height: 6'3"  Weight: 210  Origin: Round 2, 2008 Draft (#72 overall)

| YEAR | TEAM | LVL | AGE | PA | R | 2B | 3B | HR | RBI | BB | K | SB | CS | AVG/OBP/SLG |
|---|---|---|---|---|---|---|---|---|---|---|---|---|---|---|
| 2016 | COL | MLB | 29 | 641 | 111 | 35 | 5 | 29 | 82 | 43 | 102 | 17 | 9 | .324/.381/.552 |
| 2017 | COL | MLB | 30 | 725 | 137 | 35 | 14 | 37 | 104 | 65 | 135 | 14 | 10 | .331/.399/.601 |
| 2018 | COL | MLB | 31 | 696 | 119 | 31 | 7 | 29 | 70 | 59 | 134 | 12 | 4 | .291/.358/.502 |
| 2019 | COL | MLB | 32 | 638 | 98 | 33 | 6 | 26 | 83 | 51 | 124 | 15 | 7 | .302/.366/.518 |

Breakout: 0%  Improve: 40%  Collapse: 10%  Attrition: 6%  MLB: 99%
Comparables: Vernon Wells, Torii Hunter, Andre Ethier

"We're encouraged by the process," Bud Black told reporters after the game. Charlie'd tested his tight, nearly-32-year-old April quad in the outfield before the game and felt pretty good. They didn't think he'd need to go on the disabled list. And in keeping with tradition, he never did; he hasn't since running into some turf toe in the spring of 2016. Offensive regression hit like a fat sack with a dollar sign on it for a long swath of the first half, but eventually Blackmon did, too. Not with quite the consistent oomph and sting as he had in his all-world 2017 campaign, mind you. But he again hit a bunch of dingers, got on base at a good clip, and led the league in runs. It was a very, very good offensive season.

To watch him in the field, however, is to know that lower half never quite got right, in April or any other month. The sprint speed and effort checked out, but the defensive metrics averted their eyes from a start-up explosion that was suddenly more of a light crackle. Greener corner pastures likely await, and with them about 95.5 million expectations for his bat to hold and carry his contract's load.

| YEAR | TEAM | LVL | AGE | PA | DRC+ | VORP | BABIP | BRR | FRAA | WARP |
|---|---|---|---|---|---|---|---|---|---|---|
| 2016 | COL | MLB | 29 | 641 | 132 | 57.4 | .350 | 4.2 | CF(138): -7.1 | 4.4 |
| 2017 | COL | MLB | 30 | 725 | 144 | 79.2 | .371 | 1.6 | CF(158): -0.1 | 6.7 |
| 2018 | COL | MLB | 31 | 696 | 123 | 37.7 | .329 | -0.6 | CF(151): -21.7 | 2.1 |
| 2019 | COL | MLB | 32 | 638 | 131 | 45.3 | .342 | 0.4 | RF -1, CF -1 | 4.1 |

*Charlie Blackmon, continued*

**Batted Ball Distribution**

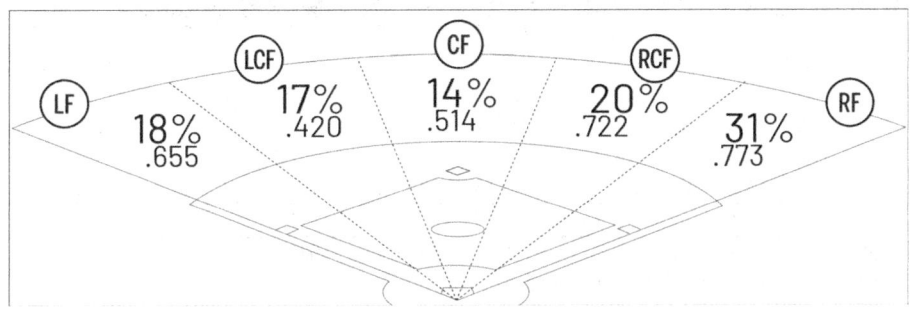

**Strike Zone vs LHP**

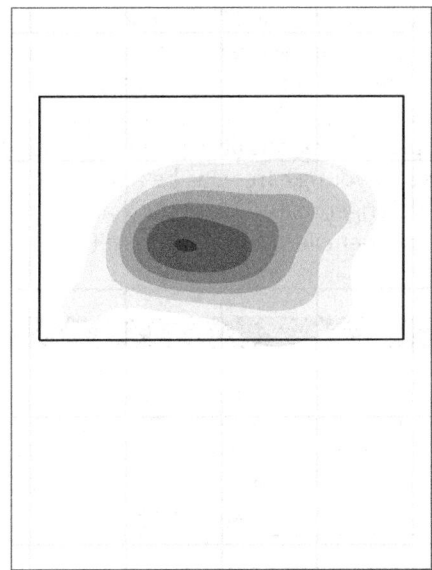

**Strike Zone vs RHP**

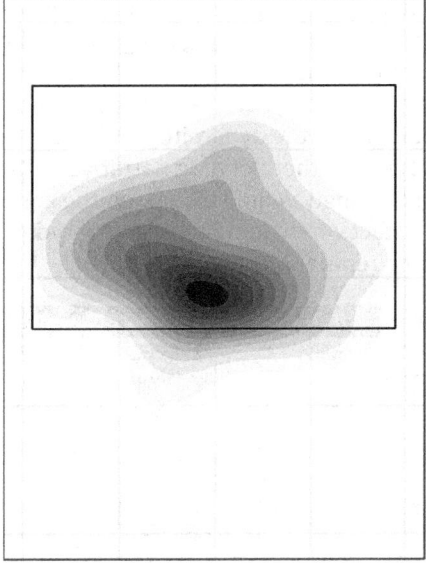

## David Dahl  LF

Born: 04/01/94   Age: 25   Bats: L   Throws: R
Height: 6'2"   Weight: 195   Origin: Round 1, 2012 Draft (#10 overall)

| YEAR | TEAM | LVL | AGE | PA | R | 2B | 3B | HR | RBI | BB | K | SB | CS | AVG/OBP/SLG |
|---|---|---|---|---|---|---|---|---|---|---|---|---|---|---|
| 2016 | NBR | AAX | 22 | 332 | 53 | 21 | 2 | 13 | 45 | 39 | 85 | 16 | 5 | .278/.367/.500 |
| 2016 | ABQ | AAA | 22 | 68 | 17 | 6 | 2 | 5 | 16 | 6 | 11 | 1 | 2 | .484/.529/.887 |
| 2016 | COL | MLB | 22 | 237 | 42 | 12 | 4 | 7 | 24 | 15 | 59 | 5 | 0 | .315/.359/.500 |
| 2017 | ABQ | AAA | 23 | 74 | 12 | 2 | 2 | 2 | 14 | 3 | 17 | 1 | 1 | .243/.274/.414 |
| 2018 | ABQ | AAA | 24 | 78 | 7 | 7 | 0 | 2 | 9 | 1 | 19 | 1 | 0 | .286/.295/.455 |
| 2018 | COL | MLB | 24 | 271 | 31 | 11 | 3 | 16 | 48 | 19 | 68 | 5 | 3 | .273/.325/.534 |
| 2019 | COL | MLB | 25 | 511 | 71 | 24 | 4 | 20 | 61 | 34 | 129 | 10 | 4 | .260/.314/.456 |

Breakout: 12%   Improve: 44%   Collapse: 19%   Attrition: 21%   MLB: 92%
Comparables: Travis Snider, Wladimir Balentien, Chase Headley

It's a tough thing, when one develops a bum rap. There's the perception, of course; impressions form in the blink of an eye, and once established they can be very difficult indeed to shake. But of perhaps greater salience, usually there's cause for it. Whither David Dahl, wearer still of the dreaded "injury prone" tag after yet *again* missing a big chunk of time, this time recovering from a broken foot that cost him two months. He returned with a roar to remind everyone of the top-shelf talent he's flashed periodically throughout his stop-and-start career. But the dynamite results came in spite of precious little progress beating back the other defining narrative of Dahl's still-young career, as he remained exceedingly willing to expand the zone and dangerously unlikely to make contact when doing so. With everyday at-bats penciled in, Colorado will hope for a reputation rehab.

| YEAR | TEAM | LVL | AGE | PA | DRC+ | VORP | BABIP | BRR | FRAA | WARP |
|---|---|---|---|---|---|---|---|---|---|---|
| 2016 | NBR | AAX | 22 | 332 | 131 | 28.6 | .351 | 3.7 |  | 1.8 |
| 2016 | ABQ | AAA | 22 | 68 | 213 | 14.4 | .543 | 0.8 | CF(11): -1.3, LF(3): 0.8 | 0.9 |
| 2016 | COL | MLB | 22 | 237 | 90 | 14.5 | .404 | 2.1 | LF(54): -2.4, CF(6): 0.3 | 0.3 |
| 2017 | ABQ | AAA | 23 | 74 | 51 | 0.2 | .294 | 0.7 | LF(6): -0.2, CF(6): -0.3 | -0.3 |
| 2018 | ABQ | AAA | 24 | 78 | 85 | -0.4 | .357 | -0.6 | RF(6): 0.2, CF(6): 0.4 | 0.1 |
| 2018 | COL | MLB | 24 | 271 | 112 | 8.4 | .311 | -1.3 | LF(34): 2.9, RF(30): -1.4 | 1.1 |
| 2019 | COL | MLB | 25 | 511 | 98 | 14.8 | .314 | 0.5 | LF 2, CF -1 | 1.6 |

*David Dahl, continued*

## Batted Ball Distribution

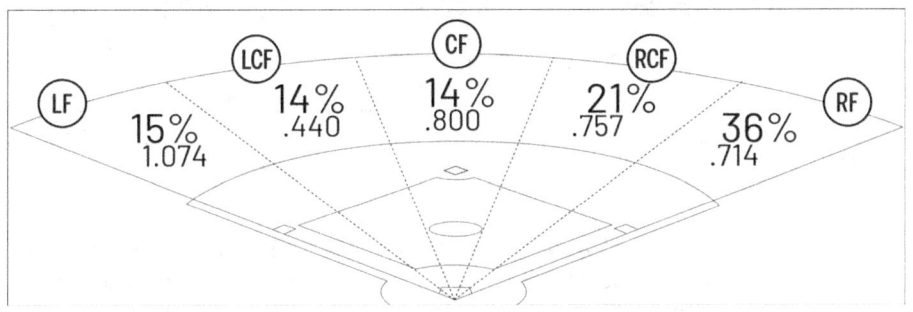

## Strike Zone vs LHP

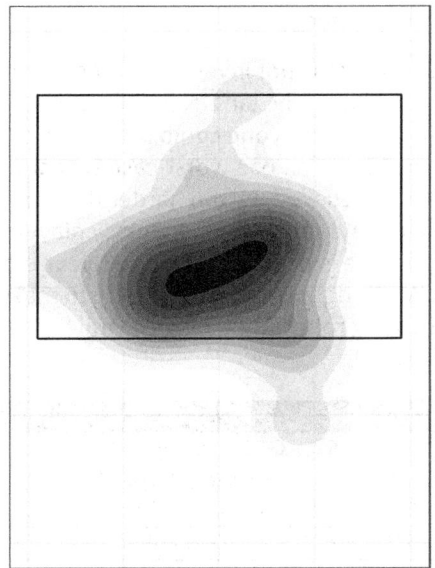

## Strike Zone vs RHP

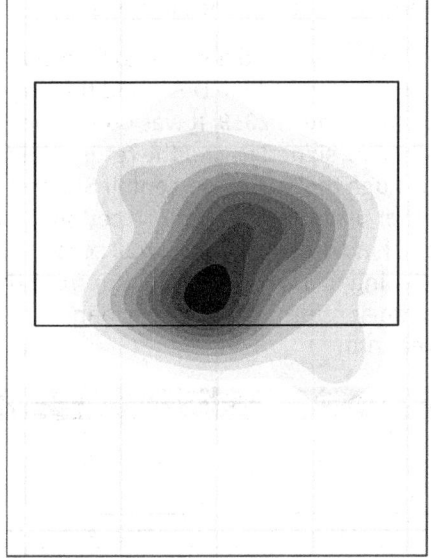

## Ian Desmond  1B

Born: 09/20/85   Age: 33   Bats: R   Throws: R
Height: 6'3"   Weight: 215   Origin: Round 3, 2004 Draft (#84 overall)

| YEAR | TEAM | LVL | AGE | PA | R | 2B | 3B | HR | RBI | BB | K | SB | CS | AVG/OBP/SLG |
|---|---|---|---|---|---|---|---|---|---|---|---|---|---|---|
| 2016 | TEX | MLB | 30 | 677 | 107 | 29 | 3 | 22 | 86 | 44 | 160 | 21 | 6 | .285/.335/.446 |
| 2017 | COL | MLB | 31 | 373 | 47 | 11 | 1 | 7 | 40 | 24 | 87 | 15 | 4 | .274/.326/.375 |
| 2018 | COL | MLB | 32 | 619 | 82 | 21 | 8 | 22 | 88 | 53 | 146 | 20 | 6 | .236/.307/.422 |
| 2019 | COL | MLB | 33 | 496 | 61 | 20 | 4 | 14 | 53 | 40 | 119 | 16 | 5 | .255/.321/.412 |

Breakout: 4%   Improve: 24%   Collapse: 24%   Attrition: 21%   MLB: 85%
Comparables: Eli Marrero, Jeff Baker, Jim Fregosi

There's this inventor from Sweden, Simone Giertz is her name. And she invents unnecessary robots. Robots that brush your teeth for you or fix you a bowl of soup. They're low on the hierarchy of robots because they don't really advance human productivity in meaningful ways. They do patch over the mundane, and that may be their greatest utility. They free up brain RAM that's otherwise committed to involuntary, procedural tasks, and that means more time to learn and create. It's not nothing, it's just not a lot of something.

Well, you'd find it easier to tie a Swedish useless robot inventor to an *Annual* comment about Ian Desmond than trying to explain the Ian Desmond contract to someone in 2019. It was one of the weirder deals anyone could remember when he signed it, and the returns have been every bit of a worst-case scenario through the first 40 percent. If Statcast is to be believed, he ran harder than any other player in the game on certain qualified plays last year and fantasy players still kind of enjoyed his 20/20 season. So all hope is not lost. But the 33-year-old is going to have to start cranking out that WARP right quick if he's going to make a run at returning any more than teeth-brushing robot value over the full five-year run.

| YEAR | TEAM | LVL | AGE | PA | DRC+ | VORP | BABIP | BRR | FRAA | WARP |
|---|---|---|---|---|---|---|---|---|---|---|
| 2016 | TEX | MLB | 30 | 677 | 100 | 26.2 | .350 | 5.5 | CF(130): -4.3, LF(29): -1.2 | 2.2 |
| 2017 | COL | MLB | 31 | 373 | 74 | 3.7 | .345 | 2.7 | LF(66): -2.8, 1B(27): -2.5 | -0.6 |
| 2018 | COL | MLB | 32 | 619 | 90 | 4.3 | .279 | 0.8 | 1B(138): -2.6, LF(18): 0.8 | 0.2 |
| 2019 | COL | MLB | 33 | 496 | 86 | 12.6 | .315 | 1.7 | CF -6, 1B 0 | 0.5 |

**Ian Desmond, continued**

**Batted Ball Distribution**

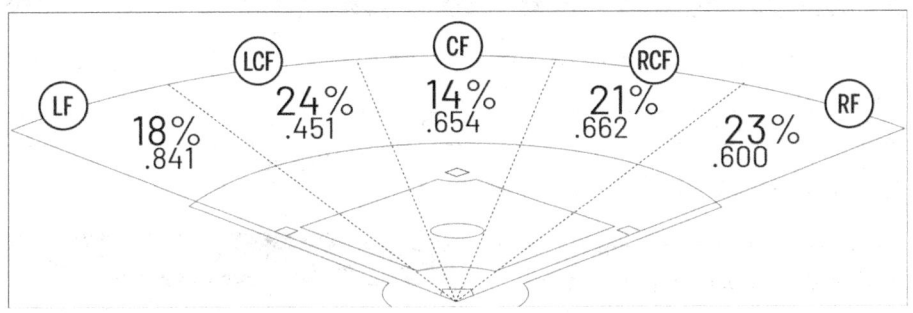

**Strike Zone vs LHP**     **Strike Zone vs RHP**

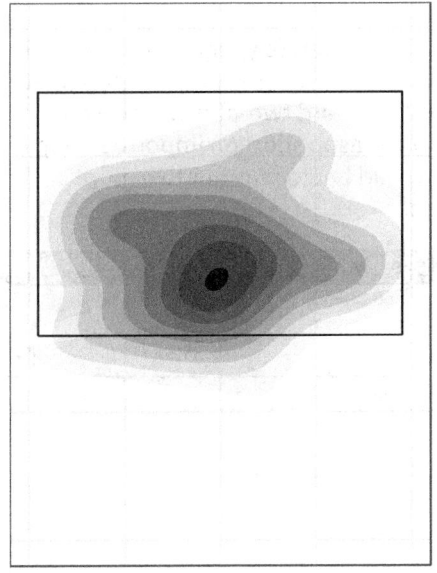 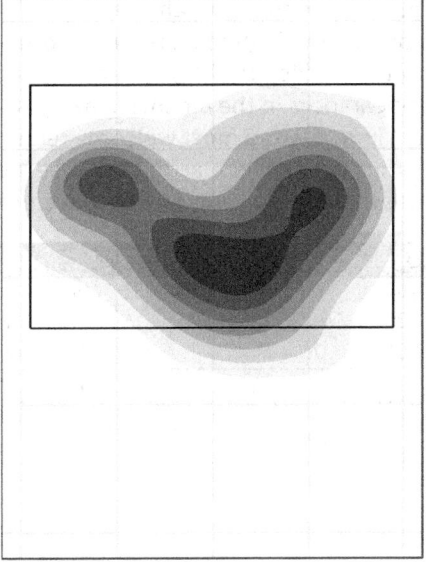

## Chris Iannetta   C

Born: 04/08/83   Age: 36   Bats: R   Throws: R
Height: 6'0"   Weight: 230   Origin: Round 4, 2004 Draft (#110 overall)

| YEAR | TEAM | LVL | AGE | PA | R | 2B | 3B | HR | RBI | BB | K | SB | CS | AVG/OBP/SLG |
|---|---|---|---|---|---|---|---|---|---|---|---|---|---|---|
| 2016 | SEA | MLB | 33 | 338 | 23 | 14 | 0 | 7 | 24 | 38 | 83 | 0 | 0 | .210/.303/.329 |
| 2017 | ARI | MLB | 34 | 316 | 38 | 19 | 0 | 17 | 43 | 37 | 87 | 0 | 0 | .254/.354/.511 |
| 2018 | COL | MLB | 35 | 360 | 36 | 13 | 1 | 11 | 36 | 50 | 87 | 0 | 0 | .224/.345/.385 |
| 2019 | COL | MLB | 36 | 331 | 39 | 16 | 2 | 10 | 39 | 38 | 83 | 0 | 0 | .245/.341/.420 |

Breakout: 1%   Improve: 26%   Collapse: 15%   Attrition: 18%   MLB: 80%
Comparables: Aaron Robinson, Ernie Whitt, Alan Ashby

The Rockies stretched Iannetta a little further than most people stretch Iannetta these days. The 13-year veteran saw as much game action as he had since 2011, though his workload behind the dish stayed a relatively consistent half-time. The starved mile-high offense, on the other hand, desperately required more of his on-base skills. He obliged by crushing a four-digit OPS in a career-high 20 plate appearances in the pinch, sneaking his way to a third two-plus win season in the last four. It was a most welcome reunion in a season short on imported happy endings in Denver. Barring collapse, he's a solid bet to play out two more reasonable-rate contract years at elevation.

| YEAR | TEAM | P. COUNT | FRM RUNS | BLK RUNS | THRW RUNS | TOT RUNS |
|---|---|---|---|---|---|---|
| 2016 | SEA | 13011 | -10.2 | -1.4 | 0.8 | -11.1 |
| 2017 | ARI | 10626 | 11.0 | -1.1 | 0.2 | 10.0 |
| 2018 | COL | 12393 | 1.4 | 0.3 | -0.4 | 1.2 |
| 2019 | COL | 11778 | 0.7 | -0.7 | 0.0 | -0.1 |

| YEAR | TEAM | LVL | AGE | PA | DRC+ | VORP | BABIP | BRR | FRAA | WARP |
|---|---|---|---|---|---|---|---|---|---|---|
| 2016 | SEA | MLB | 33 | 338 | 82 | 0.2 | .266 | -5.1 | C(93): -12.0 | -0.9 |
| 2017 | ARI | MLB | 34 | 316 | 111 | 26.2 | .308 | -2.0 | C(78): 11.2, 3B(1): 0.0 | 2.9 |
| 2018 | COL | MLB | 35 | 360 | 100 | 9.1 | .275 | -0.4 | C(99): -0.5 | 1.7 |
| 2019 | COL | MLB | 36 | 331 | 102 | 14.2 | .308 | -0.6 | C -3 | 1.1 |

*Chris Iannetta, continued*

**Batted Ball Distribution**

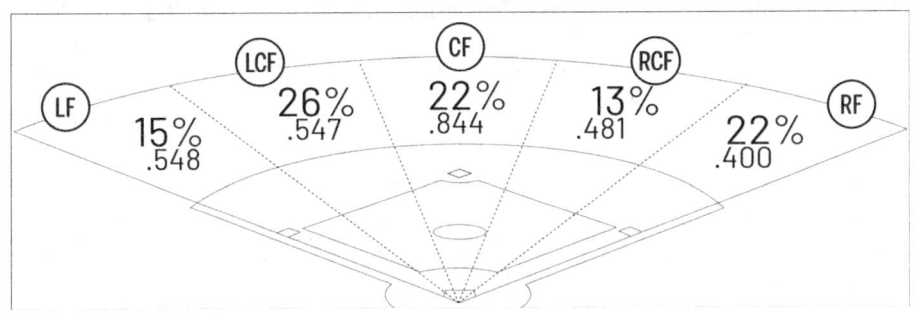

**Strike Zone vs LHP**  **Strike Zone vs RHP**

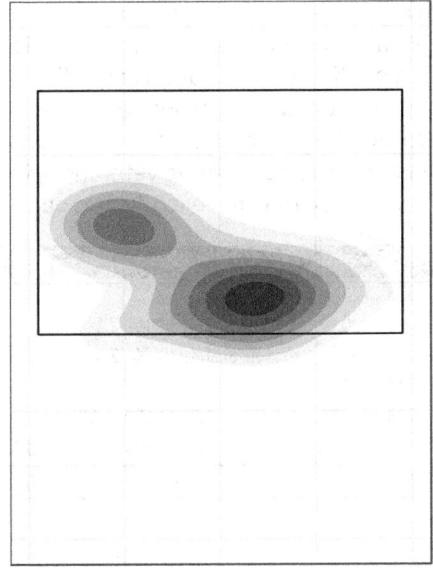 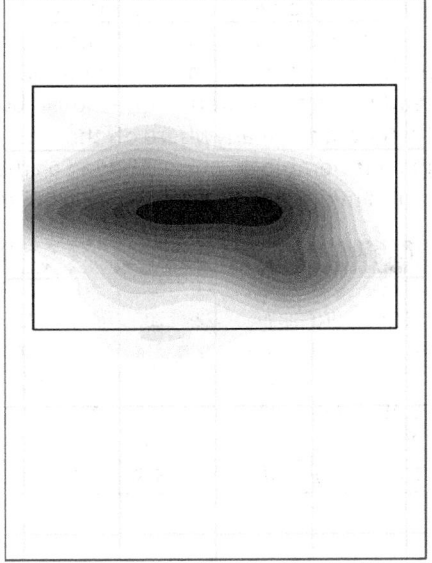

## Ryan McMahon  INF

Born: 12/14/94  Age: 24  Bats: L  Throws: R
Height: 6'2"  Weight: 185  Origin: Round 2, 2013 Draft (#42 overall)

| YEAR | TEAM | LVL | AGE | PA | R | 2B | 3B | HR | RBI | BB | K | SB | CS | AVG/OBP/SLG |
|---|---|---|---|---|---|---|---|---|---|---|---|---|---|---|
| 2016 | NBR | AAX | 21 | 535 | 49 | 27 | 5 | 12 | 75 | 55 | 161 | 11 | 6 | .242/.325/.399 |
| 2017 | HFD | AA | 22 | 205 | 28 | 16 | 2 | 6 | 32 | 20 | 39 | 7 | 0 | .326/.390/.536 |
| 2017 | ABQ | AAA | 22 | 314 | 46 | 23 | 2 | 14 | 56 | 21 | 53 | 4 | 3 | .374/.411/.612 |
| 2017 | COL | MLB | 22 | 24 | 2 | 1 | 0 | 0 | 1 | 5 | 5 | 0 | 0 | .158/.333/.211 |
| 2018 | ABQ | AAA | 23 | 242 | 40 | 15 | 3 | 11 | 48 | 15 | 61 | 3 | 2 | .290/.339/.531 |
| 2018 | COL | MLB | 23 | 202 | 17 | 9 | 1 | 5 | 19 | 18 | 64 | 1 | 0 | .232/.307/.376 |
| 2019 | COL | MLB | 24 | 479 | 57 | 27 | 3 | 17 | 60 | 32 | 128 | 4 | 2 | .260/.313/.451 |

Breakout: 8%  Improve: 36%  Collapse: 4%  Attrition: 30%  MLB: 52%
Comparables: Nick Evans, Joey Votto, Brett Wallace

McMahon's been a tough nut to crack at times, a shape-shifter in body, hitting skill development and defensive geography. It hasn't been linear, despite the straight and aggressive trajectory to Denver. Stop us if you've heard this before, but Colorado never quite committed to giving McMahon a shot at rolling into everyday reps. The bat bided time during its multiple exposures to more Triple-A pitching, and he can pick grounders at three different positions. He's still ready. There are enough questions about the hit tool and whether he can be better than fine anywhere off the coldest corner, but he remains a young player of considerable promise. So long as the Rockies continue signing veterans aging out of middle infield spots to occupy said corner, we may never truly find out.

| YEAR | TEAM | LVL | AGE | PA | DRC+ | VORP | BABIP | BRR | FRAA | WARP |
|---|---|---|---|---|---|---|---|---|---|---|
| 2016 | NBR | AAX | 21 | 535 | 94 | 14.7 | .338 | 1.3 | | 0.1 |
| 2017 | HFD | AA | 22 | 205 | 140 | 15.9 | .381 | 0.0 | 1B(25): 0.4, 2B(15): 2.1 | 1.3 |
| 2017 | ABQ | AAA | 22 | 314 | 155 | 24.7 | .416 | -2.9 | 1B(36): 1.1, 2B(24): 2.4 | 2.2 |
| 2017 | COL | MLB | 22 | 24 | 76 | 0.3 | .214 | 1.4 | 1B(7): 0.2, 2B(4): 0.0 | 0.1 |
| 2018 | ABQ | AAA | 23 | 242 | 107 | 5.6 | .353 | 1.9 | 1B(43): -1.9, 2B(10): -1.0 | 0.2 |
| 2018 | COL | MLB | 23 | 202 | 74 | -0.2 | .327 | 0.9 | 1B(31): -1.1, 3B(17): 0.1 | -0.1 |
| 2019 | COL | MLB | 24 | 479 | 100 | 17.5 | .327 | -0.2 | 2B 4, 1B -1 | 1.9 |

*Ryan McMahon, continued*

## Batted Ball Distribution

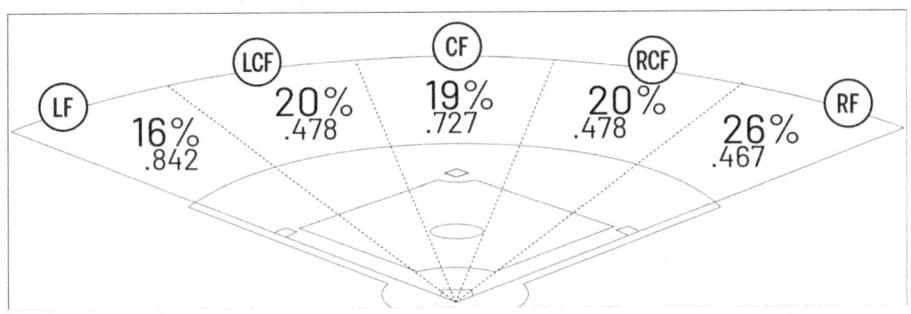

### Strike Zone vs LHP        Strike Zone vs RHP

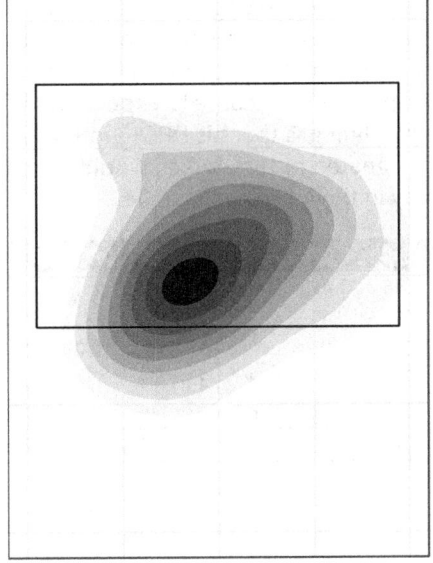

## Daniel Murphy 1B

Born: 04/01/85   Age: 34   Bats: L   Throws: R
Height: 6'1"   Weight: 221   Origin: Round 13, 2006 Draft (#394 overall)

| YEAR | TEAM | LVL | AGE | PA | R | 2B | 3B | HR | RBI | BB | K | SB | CS | AVG/OBP/SLG |
|---|---|---|---|---|---|---|---|---|---|---|---|---|---|---|
| 2016 | WAS | MLB | 31 | 582 | 88 | 47 | 5 | 25 | 104 | 35 | 57 | 5 | 3 | .347/.390/.595 |
| 2017 | WAS | MLB | 32 | 593 | 94 | 43 | 3 | 23 | 93 | 52 | 77 | 2 | 0 | .322/.384/.543 |
| 2018 | HAR | AA | 33 | 44 | 8 | 2 | 0 | 2 | 7 | 6 | 4 | 0 | 0 | .243/.364/.459 |
| 2018 | WAS | MLB | 33 | 205 | 17 | 9 | 0 | 6 | 29 | 13 | 17 | 1 | 0 | .300/.341/.442 |
| 2018 | CHN | MLB | 33 | 146 | 23 | 6 | 0 | 6 | 13 | 7 | 23 | 2 | 0 | .297/.329/.471 |
| 2019 | COL | MLB | 34 | 561 | 71 | 39 | 4 | 20 | 79 | 44 | 78 | 3 | 1 | .317/.374/.528 |

Breakout: 0%   Improve: 34%   Collapse: 19%   Attrition: 10%   MLB: 90%
Comparables: Del Pratt, Ian Kinsler, Robinson Cano

Murphy's recovery from offseason knee surgery turned out to be as frustrating as the teams he played for. Positive noises about his availability for Opening Day became muffled and then faded completely when it became apparent Murphy still wasn't able to run in March. Even when he finally did return in mid-June, he was still not starting games at second base due to concern over the knee. There aren't many major league roster spots available for bat-only players and Murphy's partial season, while respectable, was not the kind of stellar offensive output we have come to expect following his late 2015 transformation. The silver lining is that his DRC+ would still have ranked sixth among regular designated hitters, which would have been great if his next few years included a stay in the American League.

| YEAR | TEAM | LVL | AGE | PA | DRC+ | VORP | BABIP | BRR | FRAA | WARP |
|---|---|---|---|---|---|---|---|---|---|---|
| 2016 | WAS | MLB | 31 | 582 | 151 | 70.7 | .348 | 1.4 | 2B(117): -5.3, 1B(21): 0.7 | 4.9 |
| 2017 | WAS | MLB | 32 | 593 | 133 | 51.5 | .341 | 1.2 | 2B(139): 3.8 | 4.8 |
| 2018 | HAR | AA | 33 | 44 | 120 | 3.6 | .226 | 0.5 | 2B(8): -0.6, 1B(2): 0.3 | 0.2 |
| 2018 | WAS | MLB | 33 | 205 | 114 | 8.1 | .302 | -1.0 | 2B(38): -2.9, 1B(14): -0.6 | 0.4 |
| 2018 | CHN | MLB | 33 | 146 | 112 | 8.0 | .318 | 0.7 | 2B(33): -1.1 | 0.6 |
| 2019 | COL | MLB | 34 | 561 | 137 | 38.2 | .341 | -0.5 | 1B 2, 2B 0 | 4.0 |

*Daniel Murphy, continued*

**Batted Ball Distribution**

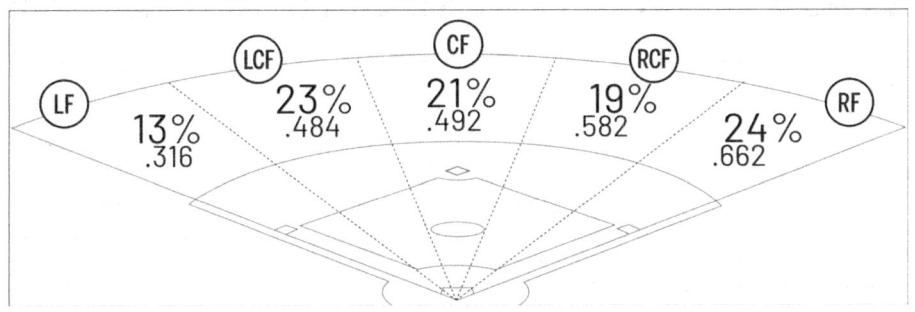

**Strike Zone vs LHP**     **Strike Zone vs RHP**

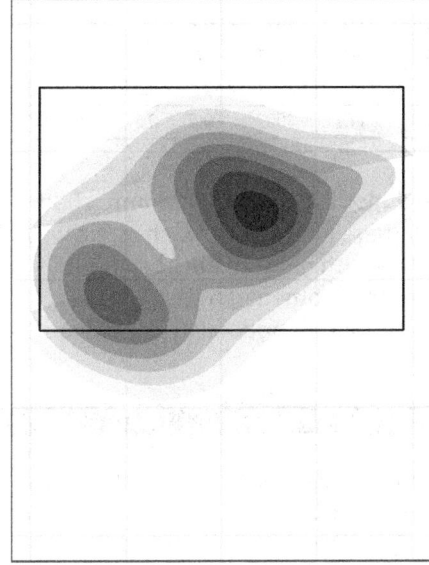
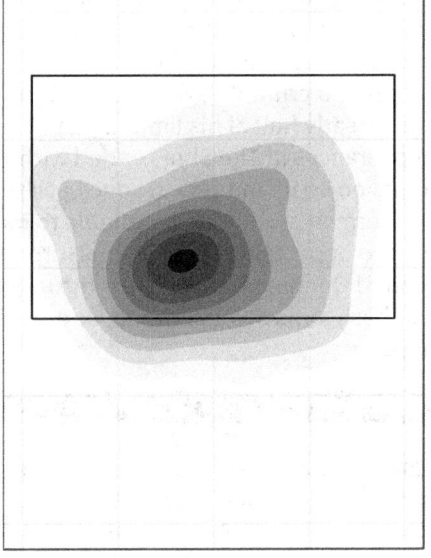

Colorado Rockies 2019

### Tom Murphy  C
Born: 04/03/91   Age: 28   Bats: R   Throws: R
Height: 6'1"   Weight: 220   Origin: Round 3, 2012 Draft (#105 overall)

| YEAR | TEAM | LVL | AGE | PA | R | 2B | 3B | HR | RBI | BB | K | SB | CS | AVG/OBP/SLG |
|---|---|---|---|---|---|---|---|---|---|---|---|---|---|---|
| 2016 | ABQ | AAA | 25 | 322 | 53 | 26 | 7 | 19 | 59 | 16 | 78 | 1 | 1 | .327/.361/.647 |
| 2016 | COL | MLB | 25 | 49 | 8 | 2 | 0 | 5 | 13 | 4 | 19 | 1 | 0 | .273/.347/.659 |
| 2017 | ABQ | AAA | 26 | 154 | 22 | 10 | 1 | 4 | 19 | 9 | 56 | 0 | 0 | .255/.312/.426 |
| 2017 | COL | MLB | 26 | 26 | 1 | 1 | 0 | 0 | 1 | 2 | 9 | 0 | 0 | .042/.115/.083 |
| 2018 | ABQ | AAA | 27 | 264 | 40 | 16 | 3 | 17 | 49 | 22 | 76 | 4 | 2 | .258/.333/.568 |
| 2018 | COL | MLB | 27 | 96 | 5 | 7 | 1 | 2 | 11 | 3 | 44 | 0 | 1 | .226/.250/.387 |
| 2019 | COL | MLB | 28 | 106 | 12 | 6 | 1 | 4 | 14 | 6 | 34 | 1 | 0 | .224/.274/.429 |

Breakout: 8%   Improve: 22%   Collapse: 8%   Attrition: 24%   MLB: 44%
Comparables: Brad Eldred, Carlos Peguero, Kelly Shoppach

They say the first step is the hardest, and in Murphy's case they've been proven largely correct, at least insofar as his trips down the first base line are concerned. Once again the backstop's bat seasoned well at Triple-A, only to wither and crumble against big-league stuff. Nearly half of his limited plate appearances in The Show ended with a shaken head and slow trudge back to the dugout. With more accomplished leathermen around and available to battery there just wasn't much in the way of earned opportunity for ol' Tom Murphy. A date with his 28th birthday right around Opening Day confirms the urgency of the moment if he's going to establish himself in Colorado, as does the one solitary option left to dot his horizon.

| YEAR | TEAM | P. COUNT | FRM RUNS | BLK RUNS | THRW RUNS | TOT RUNS |
|---|---|---|---|---|---|---|
| 2016 | COL | 1415 | 0.3 | 0.1 | 0.1 | 0.4 |
| 2017 | ABQ | 4911 | -0.8 | 0.1 | 0.4 | -0.5 |
| 2017 | COL | 1031 | -0.3 | 0.6 | -0.1 | 0.1 |
| 2018 | ABQ | 7423 | 3.8 | 1.0 | -0.2 | 4.6 |
| 2018 | COL | 2791 | -0.3 | 0.0 | 0.0 | -0.3 |
| 2019 | COL | 4009 | -0.5 | 0.2 | 0.0 | -0.3 |

| YEAR | TEAM | LVL | AGE | PA | DRC+ | VORP | BABIP | BRR | FRAA | WARP |
|---|---|---|---|---|---|---|---|---|---|---|
| 2016 | ABQ | AAA | 25 | 322 | 149 | 31.6 | .386 | -2.2 | C(69): 2.0 | 2.5 |
| 2016 | COL | MLB | 25 | 49 | 91 | 2.8 | .350 | -0.7 | C(12): 0.5 | 0.1 |
| 2017 | ABQ | AAA | 26 | 154 | 66 | 1.1 | .390 | -0.7 | C(34): 0.9 | 0.0 |
| 2017 | COL | MLB | 26 | 26 | 54 | -2.7 | .067 | 0.2 | C(8): 0.5 | 0.1 |
| 2018 | ABQ | AAA | 27 | 264 | 109 | 18.0 | .306 | -0.9 | C(52): 6.9 | 1.7 |
| 2018 | COL | MLB | 27 | 96 | 45 | -2.1 | .404 | -0.7 | C(22): -0.3 | -0.3 |
| 2019 | COL | MLB | 28 | 106 | 88 | 3.4 | .306 | -0.1 | C 0 | 0.2 |

**Tom Murphy, continued**

## Batted Ball Distribution

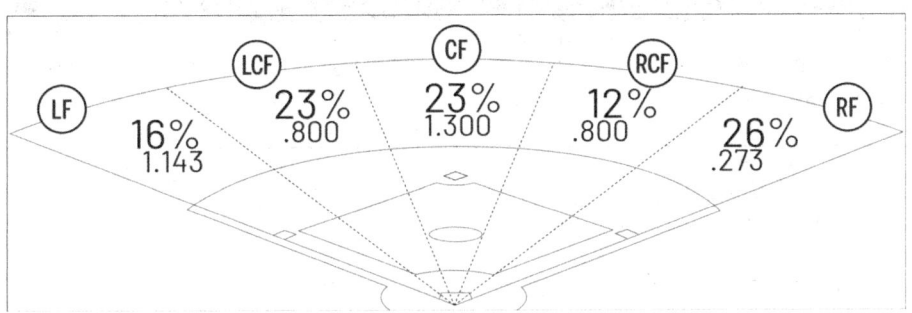

| | Strike Zone vs LHP | Strike Zone vs RHP |

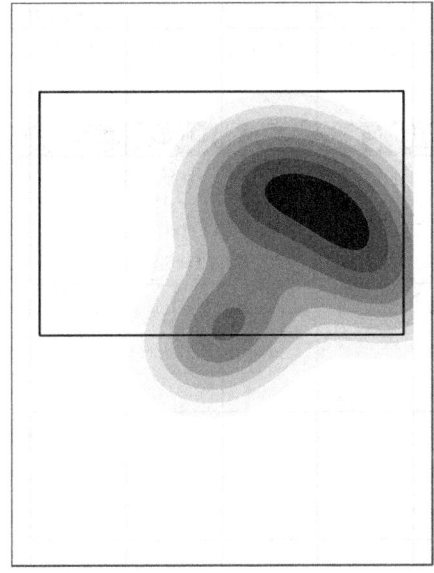 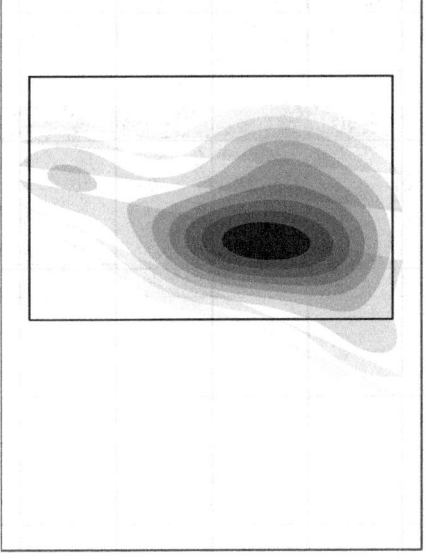

## Mark Reynolds  1B

Born: 08/03/83   Age: 35   Bats: R   Throws: R
Height: 6'2"   Weight: 220   Origin: Round 16, 2004 Draft (#476 overall)

| YEAR | TEAM | LVL | AGE | PA | R | 2B | 3B | HR | RBI | BB | K | SB | CS | AVG/OBP/SLG |
|---|---|---|---|---|---|---|---|---|---|---|---|---|---|---|
| 2016 | COL | MLB | 32 | 441 | 61 | 24 | 0 | 14 | 53 | 42 | 112 | 1 | 2 | .282/.356/.450 |
| 2017 | COL | MLB | 33 | 593 | 82 | 22 | 1 | 30 | 97 | 69 | 175 | 2 | 1 | .267/.352/.487 |
| 2018 | SYR | AAA | 34 | 42 | 3 | 1 | 0 | 1 | 4 | 3 | 13 | 0 | 0 | .231/.286/.333 |
| 2018 | WAS | MLB | 34 | 235 | 26 | 8 | 0 | 13 | 40 | 24 | 64 | 0 | 0 | .248/.328/.476 |
| 2019 | COL | MLB | 35 | 34 | 4 | 2 | 0 | 1 | 4 | 3 | 10 | 0 | 0 | .267/.333/.433 |

Breakout: 0%   Improve: 21%   Collapse: 29%   Attrition: 20%   MLB: 78%
Comparables: Eric Hinske, Chili Davis, Jeff Baker

A newly issued baseball card might tell you that only five players have popped 10 dingers in every season since 2007: Albert Pujols, Edwin Encarnacion, Jose Bautista, Robinson Cano and Reynolds. An up-to-date baseball analysis website might inform you that only one player ever has logged 6,000 major-league plate appearances with a strikeout rate over 30 percent: Reynolds. Or maybe the baseball card would tell you about the strikeout rate, and the website about the homers. The truth is blind, after all. It doesn't even know that it's sneaking up on you.

| YEAR | TEAM | LVL | AGE | PA | DRC+ | VORP | BABIP | BRR | FRAA | WARP |
|---|---|---|---|---|---|---|---|---|---|---|
| 2016 | COL | MLB | 32 | 441 | 94 | 8.9 | .361 | -2.6 | 1B(115): 1.6, 2B(1): 0.0 | 0.2 |
| 2017 | COL | MLB | 33 | 593 | 110 | 18.3 | .343 | -2.9 | 1B(138): -11.9, LF(1): 0.0 | 0.1 |
| 2018 | SYR | AAA | 34 | 42 | 55 | -0.7 | .320 | 0.2 | LF(5): 0.0, 3B(2): 0.0 | -0.1 |
| 2018 | WAS | MLB | 34 | 235 | 106 | 5.2 | .288 | -2.8 | 1B(45): -2.1, 3B(10): 0.2 | 0.1 |
| 2019 | COL | MLB | 35 | 34 | 102 | 0.6 | .335 | -0.1 | 1B -1 | 0.0 |

*Mark Reynolds, continued*

## Batted Ball Distribution

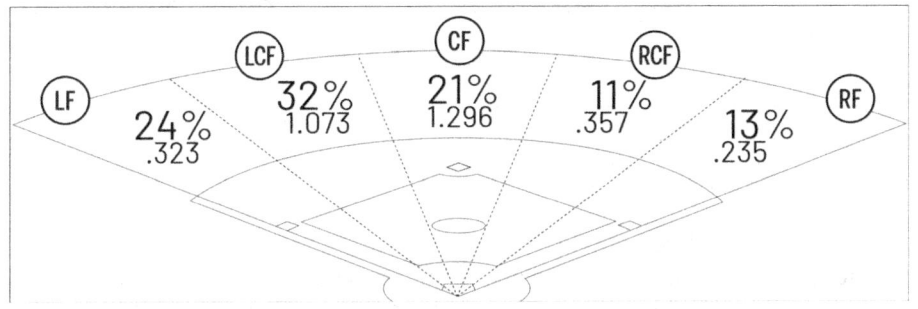

## Strike Zone vs LHP

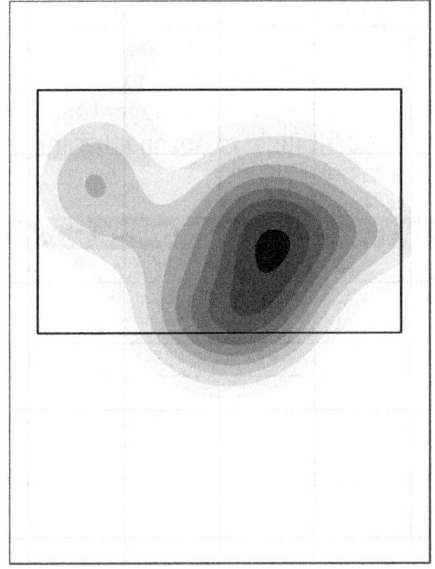

## Strike Zone vs RHP

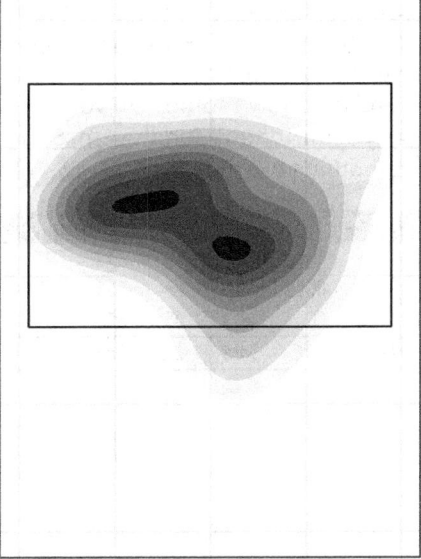

## Trevor Story  SS

Born: 11/15/92   Age: 26   Bats: R   Throws: R
Height: 6'1"   Weight: 210   Origin: Round 1, 2011 Draft (#45 overall)

| YEAR | TEAM | LVL | AGE | PA | R | 2B | 3B | HR | RBI | BB | K | SB | CS | AVG/OBP/SLG |
|---|---|---|---|---|---|---|---|---|---|---|---|---|---|---|
| 2016 | COL | MLB | 23 | 415 | 67 | 21 | 4 | 27 | 72 | 35 | 130 | 8 | 5 | .272/.341/.567 |
| 2017 | COL | MLB | 24 | 555 | 68 | 32 | 3 | 24 | 82 | 49 | 191 | 7 | 2 | .239/.308/.457 |
| 2018 | COL | MLB | 25 | 656 | 88 | 42 | 6 | 37 | 108 | 47 | 168 | 27 | 6 | .291/.348/.567 |
| 2019 | COL | MLB | 26 | 589 | 81 | 32 | 5 | 26 | 83 | 50 | 169 | 17 | 5 | .262/.330/.489 |

Breakout: 5%   Improve: 50%   Collapse: 6%   Attrition: 5%   MLB: 100%
Comparables: Mark Reynolds, Alex Rodriguez, Jason Bay

Well, now! Quite a different tale when told by a guy who's not battling a shoulder injury and striking out in over a third of his plate appearances, eh? Story hit the ball harder and did so much more frequently in 2018, shaving nearly nine percentage points off his whiff rate en route to a monster offensive campaign that was among the best in baseball, even when adjusted for the fictions of Coors. He authored significant adjustments, among them a new and pronounced early-count aggression and swing tweaks to get shorter into the zone again with the help of his longtime hitting coach. Near-elite speed gained novel utility on the bases, and the leather shone just shiny enough to justify the six and lock down some MVP votes. After dodging a late-season dagger that nearly spun Tommy John's yarn, Story will board his flight to Arizona this spring with nothing but a legend to grow.

| YEAR | TEAM | LVL | AGE | PA | DRC+ | VORP | BABIP | BRR | FRAA | WARP |
|---|---|---|---|---|---|---|---|---|---|---|
| 2016 | COL | MLB | 23 | 415 | 110 | 31.2 | .343 | 2.1 | SS(96): 0.8 | 2.7 |
| 2017 | COL | MLB | 24 | 555 | 92 | 28.7 | .332 | 4.2 | SS(142): -0.4 | 2.4 |
| 2018 | COL | MLB | 25 | 656 | 128 | 51.9 | .345 | -0.8 | SS(156): -2.0 | 5.0 |
| 2019 | COL | MLB | 26 | 589 | 108 | 31.5 | .333 | 1.7 | SS -2 | 2.8 |

*Trevor Story, continued*

**Batted Ball Distribution**

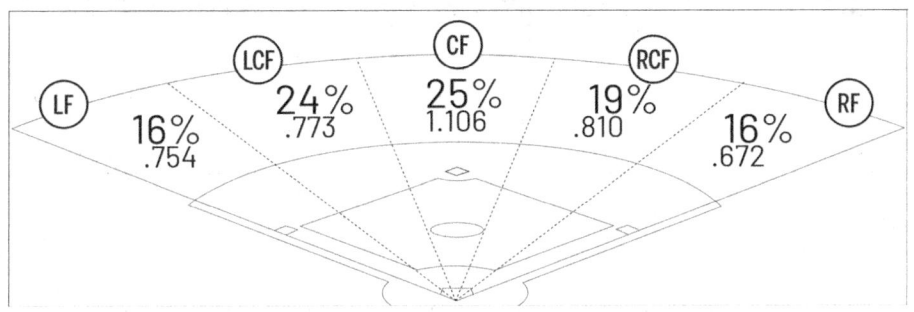

**Strike Zone vs LHP**　　　　　**Strike Zone vs RHP**

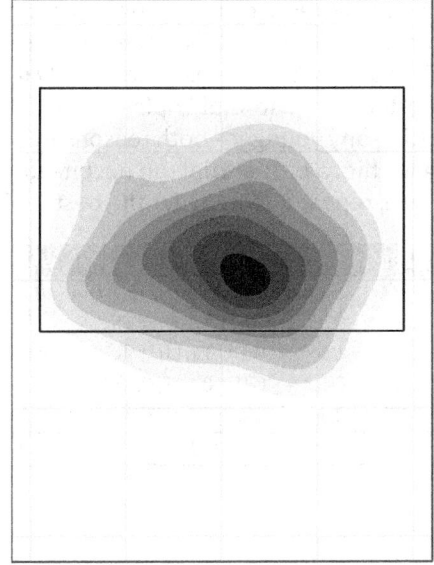 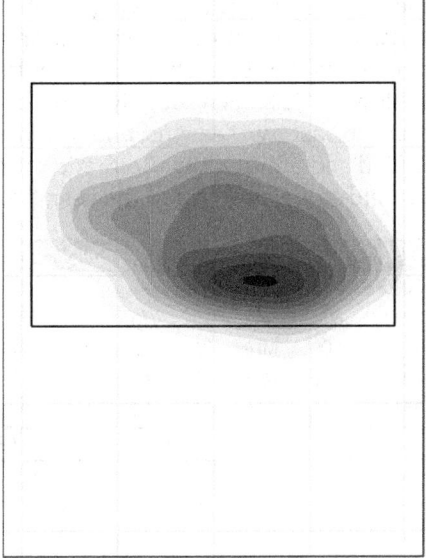

## Mike Tauchman  OF

Born: 12/03/90   Age: 28   Bats: L   Throws: L
Height: 6'2"   Weight: 200   Origin: Round 10, 2013 Draft (#289 overall)

| YEAR | TEAM | LVL | AGE | PA | R | 2B | 3B | HR | RBI | BB | K | SB | CS | AVG/OBP/SLG |
|---|---|---|---|---|---|---|---|---|---|---|---|---|---|---|
| 2016 | ABQ | AAA | 25 | 527 | 72 | 24 | 7 | 1 | 51 | 40 | 77 | 23 | 10 | .286/.342/.373 |
| 2017 | ABQ | AAA | 26 | 475 | 82 | 30 | 8 | 16 | 80 | 40 | 73 | 16 | 7 | .331/.386/.555 |
| 2017 | COL | MLB | 26 | 32 | 2 | 0 | 1 | 0 | 2 | 5 | 10 | 1 | 2 | .222/.344/.296 |
| 2018 | COL | MLB | 27 | 37 | 5 | 1 | 0 | 0 | 0 | 4 | 15 | 1 | 0 | .094/.194/.125 |
| 2018 | ABQ | AAA | 27 | 471 | 84 | 26 | 7 | 20 | 81 | 60 | 70 | 12 | 10 | .323/.408/.571 |
| 2019 | COL | MLB | 28 | 100 | 12 | 5 | 1 | 3 | 12 | 9 | 20 | 2 | 1 | .256/.327/.433 |

Breakout: 2%   Improve: 15%   Collapse: 5%   Attrition: 23%   MLB: 39%
Comparables: Kevin Thompson, Matt Angle, Craig Gentry

Tauchman absolutely *crushed* baseballs all year in Albuquerque, again, going pretty much wire to wire showcasing an impressive ability to build off of successful adjustments made the season prior. He still batters it into the dirt a ton, but he'll also loft and drive the ball away from him now or turn it loose ahead in the count. There's legitimate pop and impressive underlying contact skills, too. That kind of a combination can make gold on the silver screen, and it can fight in the "Launch Angle Revolution" as a valuable late-bloomer, if only it is allowed. He's been roughly 40-percent better than a normal Triple-A hitter over the past two seasons, and he ain't getting any younger—both reasons it baffled and amazed that Colorado never gave him a proper trial run despite dire outfield straits for most of the year. He'll rinse, repeat and hope for the best.

| YEAR | TEAM | LVL | AGE | PA | DRC+ | VORP | BABIP | BRR | FRAA | WARP |
|---|---|---|---|---|---|---|---|---|---|---|
| 2016 | ABQ | AAA | 25 | 527 | 78 | 11.1 | .337 | 5.4 | CF(93): 2.4, LF(21): 5.1 | 0.7 |
| 2017 | ABQ | AAA | 26 | 475 | 127 | 35.8 | .361 | 2.5 | CF(62): 1.3, LF(34): 5.7 | 3.2 |
| 2017 | COL | MLB | 26 | 32 | 64 | -1.0 | .353 | -0.5 | LF(3): -0.1, CF(3): -0.3 | -0.2 |
| 2018 | COL | MLB | 27 | 37 | 52 | -3.5 | .176 | 0.1 | CF(5): -0.1, LF(3): -0.9 | -0.2 |
| 2018 | ABQ | AAA | 27 | 471 | 146 | 39.6 | .345 | 3.5 | CF(65): 4.2, LF(30): 6.1 | 4.8 |
| 2019 | COL | MLB | 28 | 100 | 98 | 2.9 | .290 | 0.0 | LF 1, RF 0 | 0.3 |

**Mike Tauchman, continued**

### Batted Ball Distribution

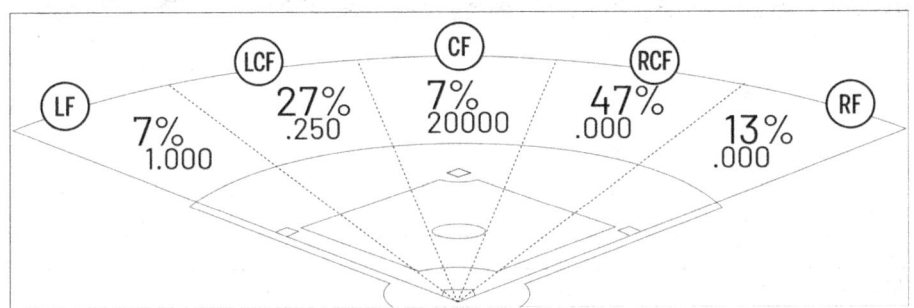

### Strike Zone vs LHP   Strike Zone vs RHP

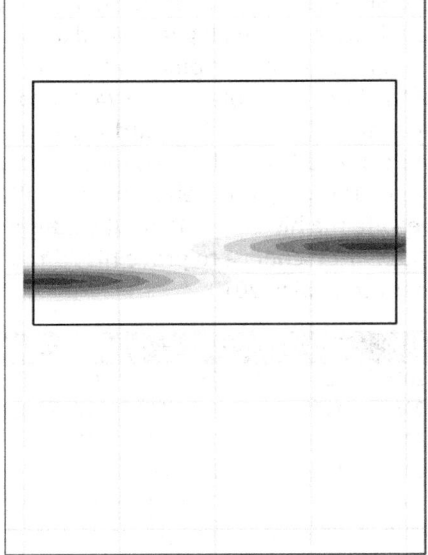

Colorado Rockies 2019

## Pat Valaika  INF

Born: 09/09/92   Age: 26   Bats: R   Throws: R
Height: 5'11"   Weight: 200   Origin: Round 9, 2013 Draft (#259 overall)

| YEAR | TEAM | LVL | AGE | PA | R | 2B | 3B | HR | RBI | BB | K | SB | CS | AVG/OBP/SLG |
|---|---|---|---|---|---|---|---|---|---|---|---|---|---|---|
| 2016 | NBR | AAX | 23 | 474 | 66 | 33 | 3 | 13 | 67 | 28 | 95 | 8 | 9 | .269/.314/.450 |
| 2016 | ABQ | AAA | 23 | 115 | 8 | 8 | 1 | 1 | 13 | 2 | 28 | 2 | 0 | .209/.226/.327 |
| 2016 | COL | MLB | 23 | 19 | 3 | 1 | 0 | 1 | 2 | 0 | 8 | 0 | 0 | .263/.263/.474 |
| 2017 | ABQ | AAA | 24 | 50 | 6 | 2 | 1 | 1 | 11 | 4 | 11 | 0 | 0 | .267/.327/.422 |
| 2017 | COL | MLB | 24 | 195 | 28 | 11 | 0 | 13 | 40 | 7 | 53 | 0 | 0 | .258/.284/.533 |
| 2018 | ABQ | AAA | 25 | 147 | 13 | 4 | 1 | 8 | 20 | 7 | 30 | 1 | 1 | .216/.252/.432 |
| 2018 | COL | MLB | 25 | 133 | 8 | 5 | 0 | 2 | 5 | 9 | 30 | 0 | 0 | .156/.214/.246 |
| 2019 | COL | MLB | 26 | 221 | 23 | 10 | 1 | 8 | 27 | 12 | 53 | 1 | 1 | .225/.274/.402 |

Breakout: 6%   Improve: 16%   Collapse: 0%   Attrition: 10%   MLB: 21%
Comparables: Wes Bankston, Kendrys Morales, Charlie Culberson

Promise turned to panic for Pat in a disastrous 2018 campaign that more than halved his once-commanding lead on the Valaika career WARP leaderboard. Of course, retaining pole position off a down year is no small feat in a family with four brothers who all got drafted and have played professional ball. But after flashing provocative pinch-hitting pop in his rookie season, the third youngest of the bunch tumbled down well below true-talent level in all hitting contexts last season, posting the third-worst OPS of any player to amass at least his 133 plate appearances. It was a most unfortunate turn of events, given a window of opportunity that somehow never really quite closed for him in Colorado. Despite the hiccup, jack-of-all-trades infield utility should afford him another shake-it-off chance to prove his 25-man mettle in a final season of pre-arbitrated team control in 2019.

| YEAR | TEAM | LVL | AGE | PA | DRC+ | VORP | BABIP | BRR | FRAA | WARP |
|---|---|---|---|---|---|---|---|---|---|---|
| 2016 | NBR | AAX | 23 | 474 | 106 | 25.9 | .315 | 2.1 |  | 1.5 |
| 2016 | ABQ | AAA | 23 | 115 | 30 | -3.3 | .265 | 0.6 | SS(15): 0.7, 2B(9): 1.5 | -0.3 |
| 2016 | COL | MLB | 23 | 19 | 68 | 0.5 | .400 | -0.4 | 3B(6): 0.1, 2B(5): -0.1 | -0.1 |
| 2017 | ABQ | AAA | 24 | 50 | 78 | 1.2 | .333 | 0.5 | SS(9): 0.3, 1B(2): 0.0 | 0.1 |
| 2017 | COL | MLB | 24 | 195 | 96 | 11.2 | .291 | 2.1 | SS(22): -0.6, 3B(19): -0.1 | 0.7 |
| 2018 | ABQ | AAA | 25 | 147 | 64 | -2.3 | .216 | -0.6 | SS(9): 0.4, 2B(9): 0.1 | -0.3 |
| 2018 | COL | MLB | 25 | 133 | 63 | -8.0 | .189 | 0.3 | 2B(17): -0.6, 1B(15): -0.4 | -0.3 |
| 2019 | COL | MLB | 26 | 221 | 72 | 0.8 | .264 | -0.3 | SS 0, 2B 0 | 0.0 |

*Pat Valaika, continued*

**Batted Ball Distribution**

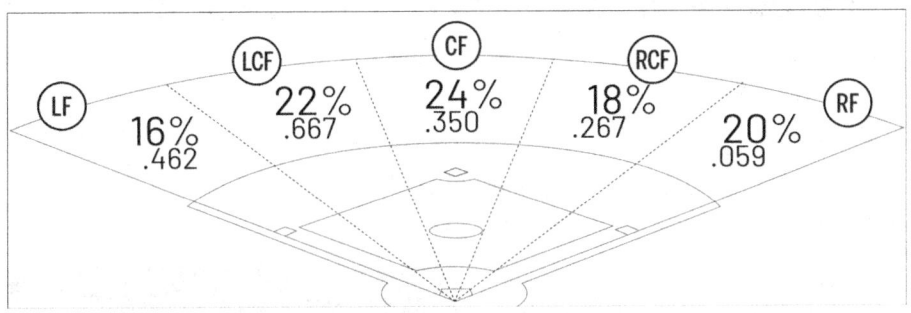

**Strike Zone vs LHP**     **Strike Zone vs RHP**

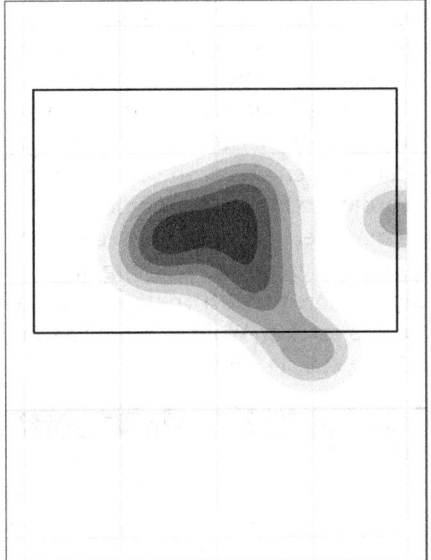

## Tony Wolters  C

Born: 06/09/92  Age: 27  Bats: L  Throws: R
Height: 5'10"  Weight: 200  Origin: Round 3, 2010 Draft (#87 overall)

| YEAR | TEAM | LVL | AGE | PA | R | 2B | 3B | HR | RBI | BB | K | SB | CS | AVG/OBP/SLG |
|---|---|---|---|---|---|---|---|---|---|---|---|---|---|---|
| 2016 | COL | MLB | 24 | 230 | 27 | 15 | 2 | 3 | 30 | 21 | 53 | 4 | 1 | .259/.327/.395 |
| 2017 | ABQ | AAA | 25 | 58 | 6 | 5 | 1 | 2 | 9 | 3 | 15 | 0 | 1 | .259/.310/.500 |
| 2017 | COL | MLB | 25 | 266 | 30 | 8 | 1 | 0 | 16 | 33 | 55 | 0 | 1 | .240/.341/.284 |
| 2018 | COL | MLB | 26 | 216 | 19 | 4 | 4 | 3 | 27 | 26 | 33 | 2 | 0 | .170/.292/.286 |
| 2019 | COL | MLB | 27 | 222 | 24 | 9 | 2 | 5 | 22 | 23 | 46 | 2 | 1 | .244/.332/.389 |

Breakout: 10%  Improve: 62%  Collapse: 10%  Attrition: 14%  MLB: 96%
Comparables: Dioner Navarro, Mickey Owen, Tom Padden

If you've ever wondered what a two-win player who hits a buck-seventy looks like, quest no further. Wolters rebounded from a concussed, sub-par effort in 2017 to post one of the league's best seasons behind the plate a year later. He's a Venus flytrap at the bottom of the zone, elite hand and wrist strength fueling a unique and devastating technique of pitch receipt that banks borderline strikes at an uncanny rate. And it's a good thing he does because when he's at the plate...well, that's usually about as far as things go. According to DRC+, the top-line numbers did overstate his struggles a bit, and he still managed to walk at an excellent rate. So there's some room to grow without even really growing. Alas, slugging under .300 for a couple years in a row despite calling Coors home'll only get you so far. The walking, framing definition of a back-up catcher, Wolters will be a fun test tube for the arbitration system over the next couple winters.

| YEAR | TEAM | P. COUNT | FRM RUNS | BLK RUNS | THRW RUNS | TOT RUNS |
|---|---|---|---|---|---|---|
| 2016 | COL | 8341 | 9.9 | -0.1 | 0.5 | 9.8 |
| 2017 | ABQ | 1747 | 2.3 | 0.0 | 0.1 | 2.6 |
| 2017 | COL | 9693 | -2.7 | -0.6 | 1.1 | -3.0 |
| 2018 | COL | 7924 | 10.2 | -0.6 | 0.2 | 9.6 |
| 2019 | COL | 8470 | 5.2 | -0.4 | 0.5 | 5.3 |

| YEAR | TEAM | LVL | AGE | PA | DRC+ | VORP | BABIP | BRR | FRAA | WARP |
|---|---|---|---|---|---|---|---|---|---|---|
| 2016 | COL | MLB | 24 | 230 | 75 | 8.4 | .336 | 0.7 | C(59): 8.9, 2B(7): -0.1 | 1.4 |
| 2017 | ABQ | AAA | 25 | 58 | 87 | 3.7 | .324 | 0.3 | C(13): 1.9 | 0.3 |
| 2017 | COL | MLB | 25 | 266 | 75 | 0.9 | .316 | 0.5 | C(77): -0.9, 2B(4): 0.1 | 0.4 |
| 2018 | COL | MLB | 26 | 216 | 76 | 1.1 | .189 | 2.5 | C(64): 10.7, 2B(2): 0.0 | 1.8 |
| 2019 | COL | MLB | 27 | 222 | 88 | 8.1 | .291 | -0.1 | C 4 | 1.1 |

**Tony Wolters, continued**

**Batted Ball Distribution**

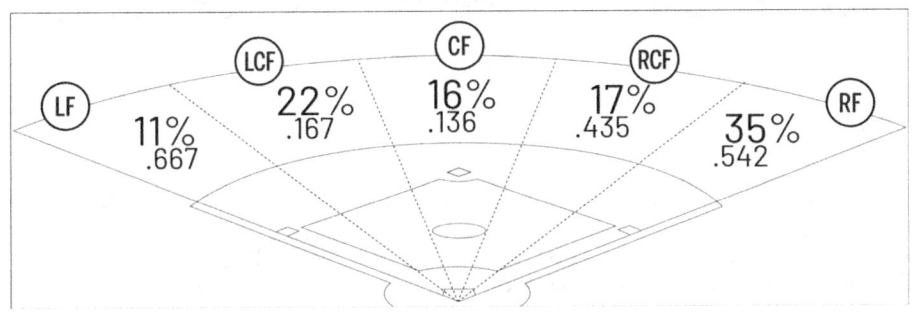

**Strike Zone vs LHP**          **Strike Zone vs RHP**

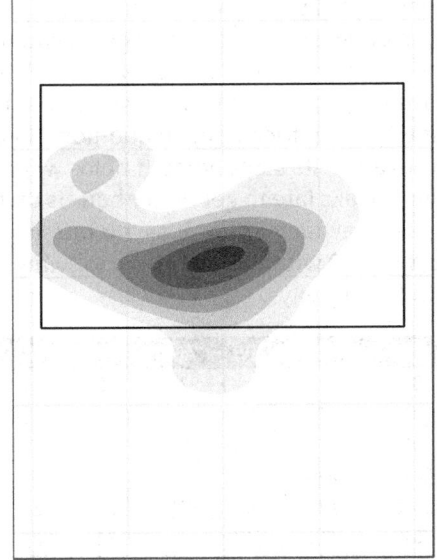

## Yency Almonte  RHP

Born: 06/04/94   Age: 25   Bats: B   Throws: R
Height: 6'3"   Weight: 205   Origin: Round 17, 2012 Draft (#537 overall)

| YEAR | TEAM | LVL | AGE | W | L | SV | G | GS | IP | H | HR | BB/9 | K/9 | K | GB% | BABIP |
|---|---|---|---|---|---|---|---|---|---|---|---|---|---|---|---|---|
| 2016 | MOD | A+ | 22 | 8 | 9 | 0 | 22 | 22 | 138$^1$ | 124 | 14 | 2.5 | 8.7 | 134 | 47% | .285 |
| 2016 | NBR | AAX | 22 | 3 | 1 | 0 | 5 | 5 | 30 | 22 | 4 | 4.8 | 6.6 | 22 | 37% | .212 |
| 2017 | HFD | AA | 23 | 5 | 3 | 0 | 14 | 14 | 76$^1$ | 58 | 4 | 3.7 | 8.4 | 71 | 45% | .267 |
| 2017 | ABQ | AAA | 23 | 3 | 1 | 0 | 8 | 7 | 35 | 41 | 7 | 5.4 | 5.7 | 22 | 50% | .321 |
| 2018 | ABQ | AAA | 24 | 3 | 5 | 1 | 18 | 10 | 43$^2$ | 44 | 8 | 2.9 | 7.0 | 34 | 45% | .283 |
| 2018 | COL | MLB | 24 | 0 | 0 | 0 | 14 | 0 | 14$^2$ | 15 | 1 | 2.5 | 8.6 | 14 | 48% | .341 |
| 2019 | COL | MLB | 25 | 2 | 2 | 0 | 15 | 5 | 35 | 36 | 5 | 3.7 | 7.9 | 31 | 43% | .296 |

Breakout: 20%   Improve: 27%   Collapse: 14%   Attrition: 34%   MLB: 54%
Comparables: Tyler Wagner, Tyler Anderson, Andrew Chafin

Showtime, indeed. One of the great transitional periods of any pitcher's baseball life is the one from proverbial thrower to proverbial pitcher. The due course of time forces every arm to confront the dichotomy at some point, and those with aspirations of starting will typically face it that much sooner. Max effort tires and joggles the fine mechanics. Almonte crossed the first bridge in that journey back at Double-A in 2017, and that stat line at Triple-A belied further gains in this past season's first half. The Rockies were convinced and lined him up for a bullpen audition. He took to the role magnificently, at least from a results standpoint. It helps when the "paired-down" heater still sits 95 and sneaks late to get under barrels on the regular. He showed the ability to coax an awful lot of whiffs with the slider, too. It's a nice starting point, and he'll enter 2019 with the versatility to swing and the stuff to impact the big-league staff in big ways.

| YEAR | TEAM | LVL | AGE | WHIP | ERA | DRA | WARP | MPH | FB% | WHF | CSP |
|---|---|---|---|---|---|---|---|---|---|---|---|
| 2016 | MOD | A+ | 22 | 1.18 | 3.71 | 3.36 | 3.3 | | | | |
| 2016 | NBR | AAX | 22 | 1.27 | 3.00 | | | | | | |
| 2017 | HFD | AA | 23 | 1.17 | 2.00 | 4.74 | 0.4 | | | | |
| 2017 | ABQ | AAA | 23 | 1.77 | 4.89 | 6.51 | -0.3 | | | | |
| 2018 | ABQ | AAA | 24 | 1.33 | 5.56 | 4.43 | 0.5 | | | | |
| 2018 | COL | MLB | 24 | 1.30 | 1.84 | 4.37 | 0.1 | 97.0 | 63 | 13.5 | 45.8 |
| 2019 | COL | MLB | 25 | 1.42 | 4.82 | 4.93 | 0.0 | 96.7 | 64.5 | 13.9 | 46.9 |

**Yency Almonte, continued**

### Pitch Shape vs LHH

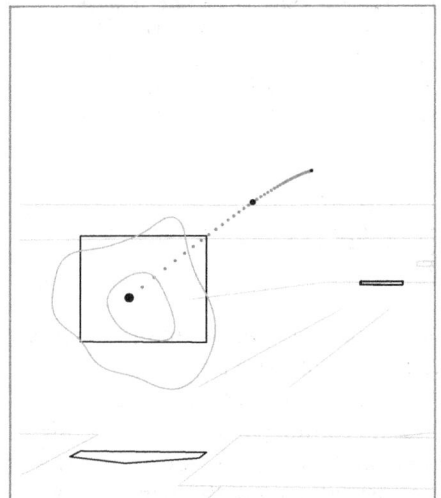

### Pitch Shape vs RHH

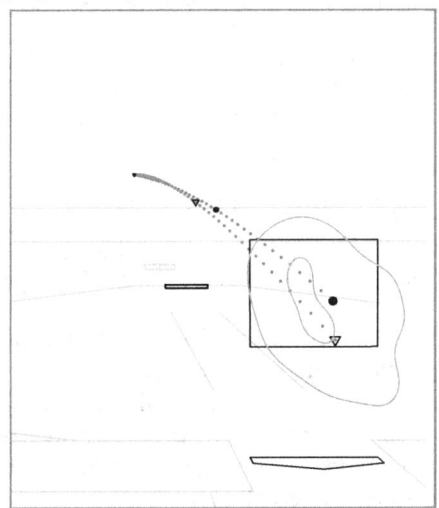

| Type | Frequency | Velocity | H Movement | V Movement |
|---|---|---|---|---|
| ● Fastball | 62.9% | 95.9 [111] | -6.7 [100] | -14.2 [105] |
| ☐ Sinker | | | | |
| + Cutter | | | | |
| ▲ Changeup | 2.4% | 88.3 [112] | -9.6 [109] | -24.5 [108] |
| ✕ Splitter | | | | |
| ▽ Slider | 34.7% | 87.7 [114] | 4 [96] | -28.8 [113] |
| ◇ Curveball | | | | |
| ⊕ Slow Curveball | | | | |
| ✱ Knuckleball | | | | |
| ▼ Screwball | | | | |

## Tyler Anderson  LHP

Born: 12/30/89  Age: 29  Bats: L  Throws: L
Height: 6'4"  Weight: 210  Origin: Round 1, 2011 Draft (#20 overall)

| YEAR | TEAM | LVL | AGE | W | L | SV | G | GS | IP | H | HR | BB/9 | K/9 | K | GB% | BABIP |
|---|---|---|---|---|---|---|---|---|---|---|---|---|---|---|---|---|
| 2016 | NBR | AAX | 26 | 1 | 1 | 0 | 2 | 2 | 10 | 6 | 0 | 1.8 | 9.9 | 11 | 59% | .222 |
| 2016 | ABQ | AAA | 26 | 1 | 1 | 0 | 3 | 3 | 17 | 15 | 1 | 3.2 | 6.9 | 13 | 48% | .286 |
| 2016 | COL | MLB | 26 | 5 | 6 | 0 | 19 | 19 | 114$^1$ | 119 | 12 | 2.2 | 7.8 | 99 | 53% | .319 |
| 2017 | ABQ | AAA | 27 | 0 | 2 | 0 | 4 | 2 | 12$^1$ | 14 | 0 | 2.9 | 9.5 | 13 | 35% | .412 |
| 2017 | COL | MLB | 27 | 6 | 6 | 0 | 17 | 15 | 86 | 88 | 16 | 2.7 | 8.5 | 81 | 46% | .304 |
| 2018 | COL | MLB | 28 | 7 | 9 | 0 | 32 | 32 | 176 | 165 | 30 | 3.0 | 8.4 | 164 | 38% | .281 |
| *2019* | *COL* | *MLB* | *29* | *9* | *8* | *0* | *24* | *24* | *136* | *134* | *20* | *2.8* | *8.5* | *129* | *43%* | *.295* |

Breakout: 29%  Improve: 46%  Collapse: 21%  Attrition: 8%  MLB: 87%
Comparables: Tommy Milone, A.J. Griffin, Zach McAllister

It took six full seasons as a professional, but Anderson finally managed to stay healthy enough to take 32 turns in Colorado's rotation. And he performed...okay! After toying with a two-seamed addition to the arsenal at season's beginning, he promptly reverted to the comfort of a three-pitch mix that includes a cutting version of both fastball and change. He found his groove in June, missed all of the barrels in July and missed none of them in August. It was a prototypical up-and-down performance from a prototypical back-end starter, the net result of which provided the Rockies 176 cheap, reasonably useful innings in sum. The arbitration clock has started ticking, so those innings will get increasingly more expensive, and a crop of higher-ceilinged young arms figures to push the former first-rounder for something a little better than "useful" in the year ahead.

| YEAR | TEAM | LVL | AGE | WHIP | ERA | DRA | WARP | MPH | FB% | WHF | CSP |
|---|---|---|---|---|---|---|---|---|---|---|---|
| 2016 | NBR | AAX | 26 | 0.80 | 1.80 | | | | | | |
| 2016 | ABQ | AAA | 26 | 1.24 | 2.12 | 3.90 | 0.3 | | | | |
| 2016 | COL | MLB | 26 | 1.29 | 3.54 | 4.88 | 0.6 | 93.7 | 43.6 | 11.4 | 48.5 |
| 2017 | ABQ | AAA | 27 | 1.46 | 4.38 | 2.92 | 0.3 | | | | |
| 2017 | COL | MLB | 27 | 1.33 | 4.81 | 4.15 | 1.3 | 93.9 | 47.1 | 12.4 | 47.6 |
| 2018 | COL | MLB | 28 | 1.27 | 4.55 | 4.82 | 1.0 | 93.7 | 44.6 | 12.3 | 50 |
| *2019* | *COL* | *MLB* | *29* | *1.30* | *4.21* | *4.39* | *1.1* | *93.1* | *44.9* | *12.2* | *48.8* |

*Tyler Anderson, continued*

### Pitch Shape vs LHH

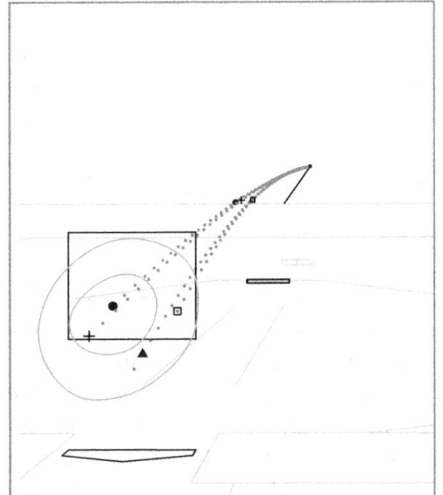

### Pitch Shape vs RHH

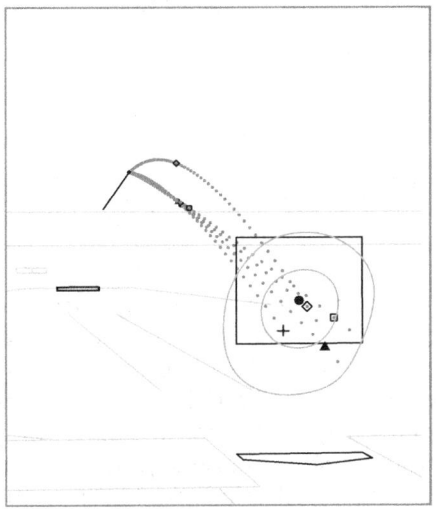

| Type | Frequency | Velocity | H Movement | V Movement |
|---|---|---|---|---|
| ● Fastball | 38.9% | 92.4 [100] | 6.6 [100] | -13.1 [108] |
| ☐ Sinker | 5.6% | 91.8 [96] | 12.5 [101] | -17.5 [109] |
| + Cutter | 28.8% | 88.1 [96] | -1.9 [100] | -22 [107] |
| ▲ Changeup | 22.9% | 81.7 [86] | 9.8 [108] | -25.8 [105] |
| ✕ Splitter | | | | |
| ▽ Slider | | | | |
| ◇ Curveball | 3.8% | 74.1 [84] | -3.1 [80] | -53 [89] |
| ⊕ Slow Curveball | | | | |
| ✻ Knuckleball | | | | |
| ▼ Screwball | | | | |

## Chad Bettis   RHP

Born: 04/26/89   Age: 30   Bats: R   Throws: R
Height: 6'1"   Weight: 200   Origin: Round 2, 2010 Draft (#76 overall)

| YEAR | TEAM | LVL | AGE | W | L | SV | G | GS | IP | H | HR | BB/9 | K/9 | K | GB% | BABIP |
|---|---|---|---|---|---|---|---|---|---|---|---|---|---|---|---|---|
| 2016 | COL | MLB | 27 | 14 | 8 | 0 | 32 | 32 | 186 | 204 | 22 | 2.9 | 6.7 | 138 | 54% | .310 |
| 2017 | ABQ | AAA | 28 | 0 | 3 | 0 | 4 | 4 | 18[2] | 22 | 2 | 2.9 | 5.3 | 11 | 55% | .312 |
| 2017 | COL | MLB | 28 | 2 | 4 | 0 | 9 | 9 | 46[1] | 52 | 8 | 2.1 | 5.8 | 30 | 50% | .293 |
| 2018 | ABQ | AAA | 29 | 0 | 0 | 0 | 3 | 3 | 14 | 16 | 2 | 1.9 | 6.4 | 10 | 51% | .311 |
| 2018 | COL | MLB | 29 | 5 | 2 | 0 | 27 | 20 | 120[1] | 121 | 18 | 3.5 | 6.0 | 80 | 51% | .280 |
| 2019 | COL | MLB | 30 | 7 | 7 | 0 | 41 | 16 | 111[2] | 122 | 16 | 3.4 | 6.3 | 78 | 50% | .299 |

Breakout: 7%   Improve: 39%   Collapse: 25%   Attrition: 11%   MLB: 79%
Comparables: Mat Latos, Jeff Niemann, Chase Anderson

A year removed from kicking cancer's ass, Bettis' single-minded focus returned to the only-marginally-less-daunting task of trying to get hitters out consistently at Coors Field. His calling card remains an ability to induce a nifty number of grounders, and best of all, the grounders he induces tend to be the weak, pulled kind that get converted into outs. Unfortunately, when hitters are able to get a little air under it these days, they lift balls harder against Bettis than just about any other pitcher in baseball. A nice April run gave way to May struggles, a horror show in middle months beset by blister issues and an eventual half-decent run of bullpen work down the stretch. That might just be a preview of coming attractions, though his barrel-scraping whiff rate suggests a treacherous path to holding down even that role.

| YEAR | TEAM | LVL | AGE | WHIP | ERA | DRA | WARP | MPH | FB% | WHF | CSP |
|---|---|---|---|---|---|---|---|---|---|---|---|
| 2016 | COL | MLB | 27 | 1.41 | 4.79 | 5.17 | 0.4 | 94.8 | 56 | 9.7 | 44.4 |
| 2017 | ABQ | AAA | 28 | 1.50 | 4.82 | 4.68 | 0.2 | | | | |
| 2017 | COL | MLB | 28 | 1.36 | 5.05 | 4.39 | 0.6 | 92.4 | 51.9 | 9.7 | 43 |
| 2018 | ABQ | AAA | 29 | 1.36 | 5.14 | 4.97 | 0.1 | | | | |
| 2018 | COL | MLB | 29 | 1.40 | 5.01 | 5.74 | -0.6 | 93.0 | 41.4 | 9.2 | 46.9 |
| 2019 | COL | MLB | 30 | 1.48 | 4.91 | 5.02 | 0.0 | 92.9 | 48.8 | 9.4 | 44.8 |

*Chad Bettis, continued*

**Pitch Shape vs LHH**

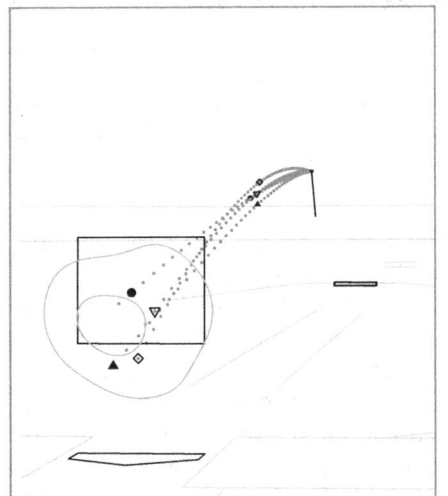

**Pitch Shape vs RHH**

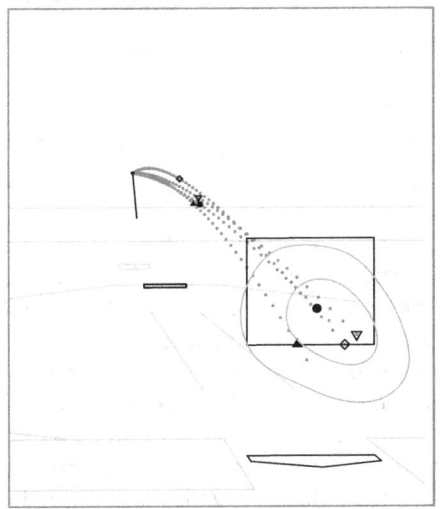

| Type | Frequency | Velocity | H Movement | V Movement |
|---|---|---|---|---|
| ● Fastball | 41.4% | 91.1 [95] | -2.9 [118] | -18.1 [93] |
| ☐ Sinker | | | | |
| + Cutter | | | | |
| ▲ Changeup | 27.4% | 86.6 [105] | -7.9 [118] | -29.1 [95] |
| ✕ Splitter | | | | |
| ▽ Slider | 18.6% | 86.5 [109] | 3.8 [95] | -27.6 [116] |
| ◇ Curveball | 12.5% | 76 [91] | 8.7 [103] | -45.1 [107] |
| ✥ Slow Curveball | | | | |
| ✱ Knuckleball | | | | |
| ▼ Screwball | | | | |

## Wade Davis    RHP
Born: 09/07/85   Age: 33   Bats: R   Throws: R
Height: 6'5"   Weight: 225   Origin: Round 3, 2004 Draft (#75 overall)

| YEAR | TEAM | LVL | AGE | W | L | SV | G | GS | IP | H | HR | BB/9 | K/9 | K | GB% | BABIP |
|---|---|---|---|---|---|---|---|---|---|---|---|---|---|---|---|---|
| 2016 | KCA | MLB | 30 | 2 | 1 | 27 | 45 | 0 | 43$^1$ | 33 | 0 | 3.3 | 9.8 | 47 | 48% | .300 |
| 2017 | CHN | MLB | 31 | 4 | 2 | 32 | 59 | 0 | 58$^2$ | 39 | 6 | 4.3 | 12.1 | 79 | 42% | .262 |
| 2018 | COL | MLB | 32 | 3 | 6 | 43 | 69 | 0 | 65$^1$ | 43 | 8 | 3.6 | 10.7 | 78 | 42% | .238 |
| 2019 | COL | MLB | 33 | 3 | 3 | 35 | 56 | 0 | 59$^1$ | 51 | 7 | 3.8 | 9.7 | 64 | 43% | .290 |

Breakout: 22%   Improve: 40%   Collapse: 36%   Attrition: 8%   MLB: 96%
Comparables: Pedro Strop, Brian Fuentes, Joe Nathan

Things went pretty well for Davis in 2018, at least under the hood. His velocity basically held, which is perhaps the nicest peg on which any hurler can hang his after-30 hat. He continued to baffle with two elite whiff-generating pitches in his cutter and curve, the latter an especially deadly weapon. And hey, 43 saves are 43 saves. But more practically speaking, the season was a bit of a slog for the $52 million man. He received a standard and unceremonious mile-high treatment, paying a 150-point OPS tax on his adopted mound. And he blew a bunch of games at the top of a house-of-cards bullpen, including some higher-profile implosions amid the growing late-summer fire devil of an NL West race. So goes the life of the ninth-inning man. Colorado will hope the results part goes a bit better next year, and the year after for that matter, even if they'll likely be satisfied with another couple seasons of more or less the same, steady skill set.

| YEAR | TEAM | LVL | AGE | WHIP | ERA | DRA | WARP | MPH | FB% | WHF | CSP |
|---|---|---|---|---|---|---|---|---|---|---|---|
| 2016 | KCA | MLB | 30 | 1.13 | 1.87 | 2.99 | 1.0 | 97.8 | 50.1 | 13.6 | 43.5 |
| 2017 | CHN | MLB | 31 | 1.14 | 2.30 | 2.78 | 1.6 | 96.1 | 47.6 | 16 | 41.8 |
| 2018 | COL | MLB | 32 | 1.06 | 4.13 | 3.90 | 0.8 | 95.5 | 49 | 12.7 | 40.1 |
| 2019 | COL | MLB | 33 | 1.28 | 3.61 | 3.88 | 0.6 | 95.1 | 48.1 | 13.9 | 41 |

*Wade Davis, continued*

### Pitch Shape vs LHH

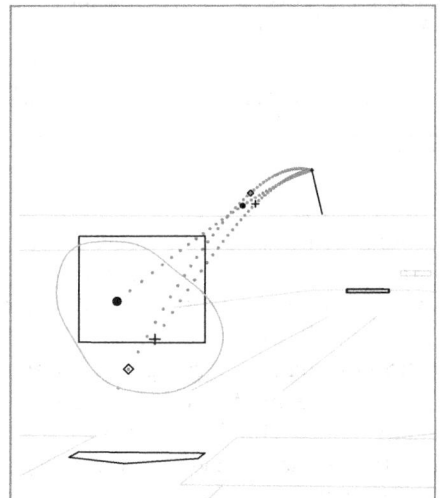

### Pitch Shape vs RHH

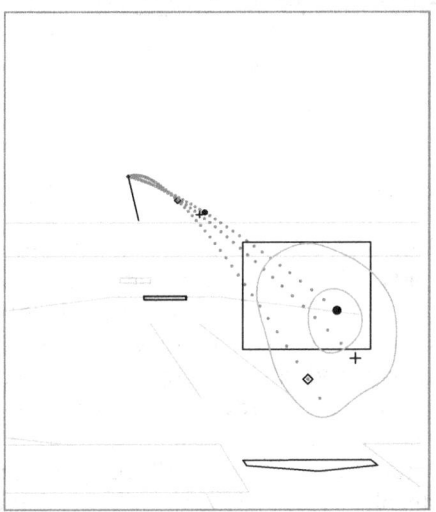

| Type | Frequency | Velocity | H Movement | V Movement |
|---|---|---|---|---|
| ● Fastball | 47.1% | 94.4 [106] | -1.4 [125] | -13.1 [108] |
| ☐ Sinker | 1.9% | 93 [103] | -9.2 [128] | -19.7 [102] |
| + Cutter | 28.8% | 90.2 [109] | 4.8 [117] | -24.2 [98] |
| ▲ Changeup | 0.5% | 91 [123] | -10 [107] | -21.6 [117] |
| ✕ Splitter | | | | |
| ▽ Slider | | | | |
| ◇ Curveball | 21.6% | 83.8 [120] | 6 [92] | -43.2 [111] |
| ⊕ Slow Curveball | | | | |
| ✻ Knuckleball | | | | |
| ▼ Screwball | | | | |

## Colorado Rockies 2019

**Mike Dunn   LHP**
Born: 05/23/85   Age: 34   Bats: L   Throws: L
Height: 6'0"   Weight: 215   Origin: Round 33, 2004 Draft (#999 overall)

| YEAR | TEAM | LVL | AGE | W | L | SV | G | GS | IP | H | HR | BB/9 | K/9 | K | GB% | BABIP |
|------|------|-----|-----|---|---|----|----|----|----|----|----|------|-----|---|-----|-------|
| 2016 | MIA | MLB | 31 | 6 | 1 | 0 | 51 | 0 | 42$^1$ | 43 | 5 | 2.3 | 8.1 | 38 | 30% | .319 |
| 2017 | COL | MLB | 32 | 5 | 1 | 0 | 68 | 0 | 50$^1$ | 43 | 8 | 5.0 | 10.2 | 57 | 34% | .276 |
| 2018 | COL | MLB | 33 | 0 | 0 | 0 | 25 | 0 | 17 | 22 | 1 | 9.5 | 6.4 | 12 | 38% | .404 |
| *2019* | *COL* | *MLB* | *34* | *1* | *2* | *0* | *31* | *0* | *32$^1$* | *35* | *5* | *4.7* | *7.4* | *27* | *37%* | *.303* |

Breakout: 19%   Improve: 35%   Collapse: 25%   Attrition: 14%   MLB: 83%
Comparables: Juan Cruz, John Axford, Will Ohman

Mmmm, you forgot about Dunn when you were mentally Rolodexing all those bad Rockie reliever contracts, didn't you? These were dark days indeed in 2018, as the veteran southpaw tweaked his throwing shoulder in off-season workouts, tried (wildly unsuccessfully) to pitch through the pain, and ultimately succumbed to surgery that mercifully cut short his miserable campaign. When he's right he'll provide serviceable depth through the middle innings. But given his fly-ball tendencies and diminished velocity it seems unlikely that even in a return to good health he'll be able to pull off the late save on what has rapidly devolved into still more sunk cost in the Colorado 'pen.

| YEAR | TEAM | LVL | AGE | WHIP | ERA | DRA | WARP | MPH | FB% | WHF | CSP |
|------|------|-----|-----|------|-----|-----|------|-----|-----|-----|-----|
| 2016 | MIA | MLB | 31 | 1.28 | 3.40 | 5.62 | -0.3 | 95.8 | 62.9 | 12.8 | 49.2 |
| 2017 | COL | MLB | 32 | 1.41 | 4.47 | 5.29 | -0.1 | 93.8 | 51.9 | 10.8 | 44.3 |
| 2018 | COL | MLB | 33 | 2.35 | 9.00 | 6.96 | -0.4 | 93.3 | 56.1 | 10.6 | 43 |
| *2019* | *COL* | *MLB* | *34* | *1.64* | *5.60* | *5.43* | *-0.2* | *93.2* | *55.2* | *11.2* | *44.3* |

*Mike Dunn, continued*

### Pitch Shape vs LHH

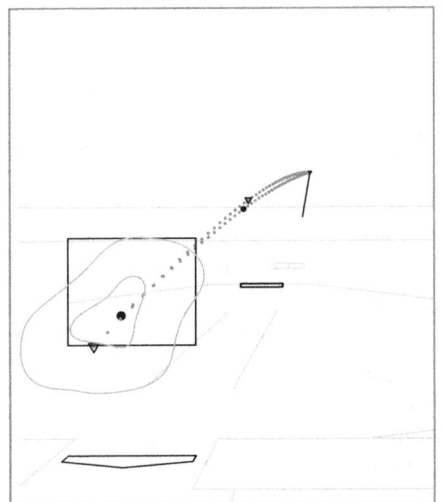

### Pitch Shape vs RHH

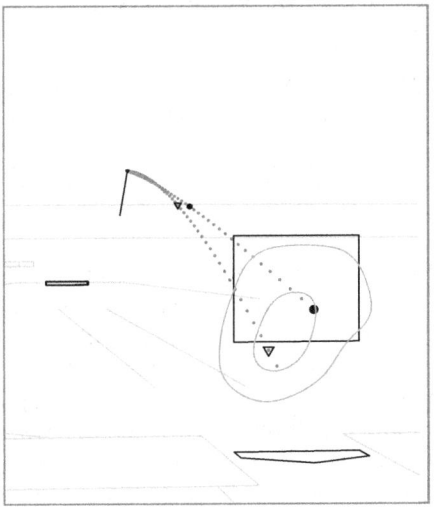

| Type | Frequency | Velocity | H Movement | V Movement |
|---|---|---|---|---|
| ● Fastball | 55.2% | 92.7 [100] | 1.6 [123] | -13.3 [108] |
| ☐ Sinker | 0.9% | 92.8 [102] | 9.5 [126] | -16.5 [113] |
| + Cutter | | | | |
| ▲ Changeup | | | | |
| ✕ Splitter | | | | |
| ▽ Slider | 36.9% | 86.3 [108] | -5.7 [103] | -28.4 [114] |
| ◇ Curveball | 7.1% | 74 [83] | -9.1 [105] | -55.9 [82] |
| ⊕ Slow Curveball | | | | |
| ✴ Knuckleball | | | | |
| ▼ Screwball | | | | |

## Kyle Freeland  LHP

Born: 05/14/93  Age: 26  Bats: L  Throws: L
Height: 6'3"  Weight: 170  Origin: Round 1, 2014 Draft (#8 overall)

| YEAR | TEAM | LVL | AGE | W | L | SV | G | GS | IP | H | HR | BB/9 | K/9 | K | GB% | BABIP |
|---|---|---|---|---|---|---|---|---|---|---|---|---|---|---|---|---|
| 2016 | NBR | AAX | 23 | 5 | 7 | 0 | 14 | 14 | 88$^1$ | 84 | 9 | 2.5 | 5.2 | 51 | 53% | .268 |
| 2016 | ABQ | AAA | 23 | 6 | 3 | 0 | 12 | 12 | 73$^2$ | 81 | 7 | 2.3 | 7.0 | 57 | 55% | .330 |
| 2017 | COL | MLB | 24 | 11 | 11 | 0 | 33 | 28 | 156 | 169 | 17 | 3.6 | 6.2 | 107 | 56% | .308 |
| 2018 | COL | MLB | 25 | 17 | 7 | 0 | 33 | 33 | 202$^1$ | 182 | 17 | 3.1 | 7.7 | 173 | 48% | .285 |
| 2019 | COL | MLB | 26 | 11 | 9 | 0 | 28 | 28 | 168 | 163 | 20 | 3.0 | 7.7 | 144 | 49% | .294 |

Breakout: 26%  Improve: 60%  Collapse: 19%  Attrition: 9%  MLB: 90%
Comparables: Martin Perez, Sonny Gray, Jesse Hahn

Skepticism is a healthy part of evaluation, but it can create lag in appreciation. Freeland's debut the season prior had been very good, as far as most of the results went. But DRA was skeptical of a pitcher who whiffed so few in such an important place and time to whiff many. His game of keeping contact off the barrel doesn't tend to maintain as regularly, you see, especially at the height of rarefied air. Well, it translated in 2018, alright. Freeland shattered the all-time ERA mark for a pitcher at Coors, solving the impossibility of altitude across 15 excellent starts. The cutter cuts an obscene amount, and by year's end he was weaving hard stuff-heavy sequencing in and out of whichever quadrants he wanted. A dominant 11-game run tied off a rare 200-inning regular season and presaged electricity in October. The Rockies will gladly take four more sequels atop their rotation, though this next one will be his last before they have to start paying for the pleasure.

| YEAR | TEAM | LVL | AGE | WHIP | ERA | DRA | WARP | MPH | FB% | WHF | CSP |
|---|---|---|---|---|---|---|---|---|---|---|---|
| 2016 | NBR | AAX | 23 | 1.23 | 3.87 | | | | | | |
| 2016 | ABQ | AAA | 23 | 1.36 | 3.91 | 3.97 | 1.2 | | | | |
| 2017 | COL | MLB | 24 | 1.49 | 4.10 | 5.91 | -0.6 | 93.6 | 64.5 | 8.2 | 46.1 |
| 2018 | COL | MLB | 25 | 1.25 | 2.85 | 3.89 | 3.3 | 93.6 | 52.5 | 9.9 | 47.9 |
| 2019 | COL | MLB | 26 | 1.30 | 4.09 | 4.26 | 1.5 | 93.2 | 58.2 | 9.4 | 48 |

*Kyle Freeland, continued*

## Pitch Shape vs LHH

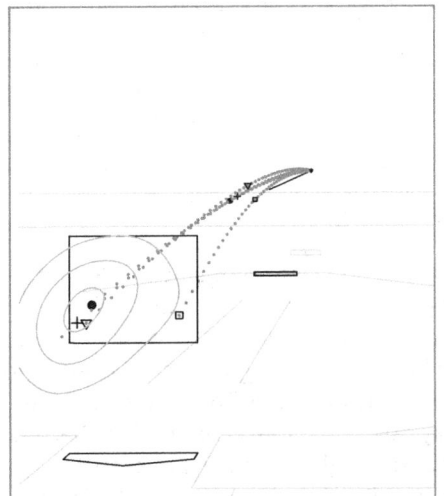

## Pitch Shape vs RHH

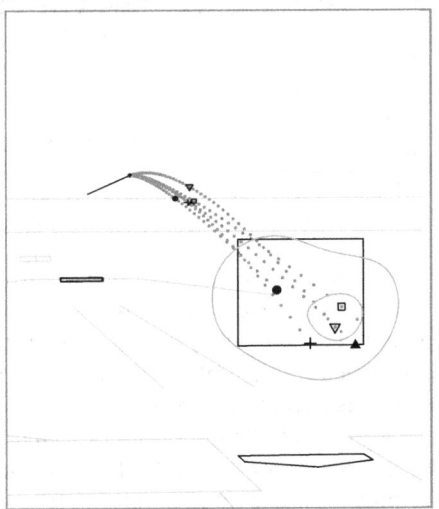

| Type | Frequency | Velocity | H Movement | V Movement |
|---|---|---|---|---|
| ● Fastball | 39.0% | 92.4 [100] | 5.6 [105] | -17.8 [94] |
| ☐ Sinker | 13.5% | 91.2 [94] | 11.6 [108] | -23.3 [90] |
| + Cutter | 27.0% | 86.5 [87] | -2.6 [104] | -27.8 [84] |
| ▲ Changeup | 13.7% | 86.1 [103] | 10 [107] | -27.9 [98] |
| ✕ Splitter | | | | |
| ▽ Slider | 6.8% | 81.7 [87] | -2.2 [89] | -35 [94] |
| ◇ Curveball | | | | |
| ⊕ Slow Curveball | | | | |
| ✳ Knuckleball | | | | |
| ▼ Screwball | | | | |

# Colorado Rockies 2019

## Jon Gray  RHP
Born: 11/05/91   Age: 27   Bats: R   Throws: R
Height: 6'4"   Weight: 235   Origin: Round 1, 2013 Draft (#3 overall)

| YEAR | TEAM | LVL | AGE | W | L | SV | G | GS | IP | H | HR | BB/9 | K/9 | K | GB% | BABIP |
|------|------|-----|-----|---|---|----|----|----|-----|-----|----|------|-----|-----|-----|-------|
| 2016 | COL  | MLB | 24  | 10| 10| 0  | 29 | 29 | 168 | 153 | 18 | 3.2  | 9.9 | 185 | 45% | .309  |
| 2017 | COL  | MLB | 25  | 10| 4 | 0  | 20 | 20 | 110$^1$ | 113 | 10 | 2.4 | 9.1 | 112 | 49% | .336 |
| 2018 | ABQ  | AAA | 26  | 1 | 0 | 0  | 2  | 2  | 10$^2$ | 7 | 1 | 3.4 | 11.0 | 13 | 63% | .231 |
| 2018 | COL  | MLB | 26  | 12| 9 | 0  | 31 | 31 | 172$^1$ | 180 | 27 | 2.7 | 9.6 | 183 | 49% | .323 |
| 2019 | COL  | MLB | 27  | 10| 7 | 0  | 26 | 26 | 148 | 139 | 16 | 2.9  | 9.4 | 155 | 47% | .305  |

Breakout: 20%   Improve: 48%   Collapse: 16%   Attrition: 4%   MLB: 88%
Comparables: Danny Salazar, Jordan Zimmermann, Jake Odorizzi

The Rockies' erstwhile Ace walked through the gates at Talking Stick a leaner man after battling foot issues the season prior. But the trimmed-down Gray never really found a tighter groove, and a grooveless summer is no way to live. The velocity trailed off across the second half as his drive got stuck in traffic and his release point fluttered on up into the thin atmosphere. The spring in his step looked sprung. Playoff purgatory's a funky position for an Opening Day Starter, but a rocky homestretch tied a bow on it and bought him bleacher seats for October. DRA expected a better fate even in spite of the stretches of struggles, though there was an awful lot of hard contact along the way. The ceiling remains significant, but if it feels like an important season ahead for Gray, it is: The arbitration clock has started cha-chinging and the top of the rotation's been reserved for others.

| YEAR | TEAM | LVL | AGE | WHIP | ERA | DRA | WARP | MPH | FB% | WHF | CSP |
|------|------|-----|-----|------|-----|-----|------|-----|-----|-----|-----|
| 2016 | COL  | MLB | 24  | 1.26 | 4.61| 4.54| 1.6  | 97.9| 55  | 13  | 48.2|
| 2017 | COL  | MLB | 25  | 1.30 | 3.67| 3.32| 2.8  | 97.8| 57.4| 9.9 | 49.8|
| 2018 | ABQ  | AAA | 26  | 1.03 | 3.38| 3.34| 0.3  |     |     |     |     |
| 2018 | COL  | MLB | 26  | 1.35 | 5.12| 4.45| 1.7  | 96.8| 49.7| 13.3| 48.7|
| 2019 | COL  | MLB | 27  | 1.28 | 3.46| 3.60| 2.5  | 96.9| 53.7| 12.5| 49.5|

*Jon Gray, continued*

### Pitch Shape vs LHH

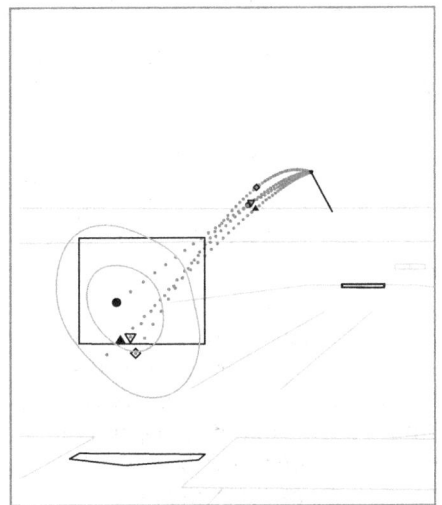

### Pitch Shape vs RHH

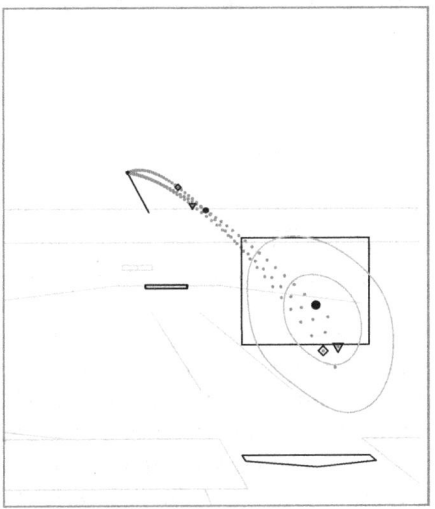

| Type | Frequency | Velocity | H Movement | V Movement |
|---|---|---|---|---|
| ● Fastball | 49.7% | 95.3 [109] | -7.5 [96] | -14.5 [104] |
| ☐ Sinker | | | | |
| + Cutter | | | | |
| ▲ Changeup | 1.7% | 87 [107] | -7.9 [118] | -21.1 [118] |
| ✕ Splitter | | | | |
| ▽ Slider | 34.0% | 88.4 [118] | 2 [88] | -24.7 [125] |
| ◇ Curveball | 14.7% | 80.2 [106] | 5.3 [89] | -42.4 [113] |
| ⊕ Slow Curveball | | | | |
| ✱ Knuckleball | | | | |
| ▼ Screwball | | | | |

# Colorado Rockies 2019

## Jeff Hoffman   RHP

Born: 01/08/93   Age: 26   Bats: R   Throws: R
Height: 6'5"   Weight: 225   Origin: Round 1, 2014 Draft (#9 overall)

| YEAR | TEAM | LVL | AGE | W | L | SV | G | GS | IP | H | HR | BB/9 | K/9 | K | GB% | BABIP |
|---|---|---|---|---|---|---|---|---|---|---|---|---|---|---|---|---|
| 2016 | ABQ | AAA | 23 | 6 | 9 | 0 | 22 | 22 | $118^2$ | 117 | 11 | 3.3 | 9.4 | 124 | 44% | .325 |
| 2016 | COL | MLB | 23 | 0 | 4 | 0 | 8 | 6 | $31^1$ | 37 | 7 | 4.9 | 6.3 | 22 | 51% | .297 |
| 2017 | ABQ | AAA | 24 | 3 | 3 | 0 | 10 | 10 | $49^2$ | 44 | 3 | 3.4 | 8.5 | 47 | 46% | .285 |
| 2017 | COL | MLB | 24 | 6 | 5 | 0 | 23 | 16 | $99^1$ | 106 | 15 | 3.6 | 7.4 | 82 | 42% | .304 |
| 2018 | COL | MLB | 25 | 0 | 0 | 0 | 6 | 1 | $8^2$ | 15 | 0 | 7.3 | 5.2 | 5 | 53% | .469 |
| 2018 | ABQ | AAA | 25 | 6 | 8 | 0 | 21 | 21 | $105^2$ | 105 | 9 | 4.0 | 8.7 | 102 | 46% | .331 |
| *2019* | *COL* | *MLB* | *26* | *3* | *3* | *0* | *10* | *10* | *53* | *52* | *7* | *3.6* | *8.0* | *47* | *44%* | *.297* |

Breakout: 25%   Improve: 46%   Collapse: 21%   Attrition: 31%   MLB: 75%
Comparables: Carlos Carrasco, Robbie Erlin, Anthony Bass

The Rockies did Toronto a big financial solid when they finally shipped Tulo in order to shop higher shelves and jumpstart their reboot. Hoffman was the spoils. Scouts loved the size, gas and hook, and Tommy John recovery was melting further into the past by the day. But it's been a minute now, and the stuff has backed up and dragged the control down with the ship. He made it back to the majors again in June, though the leash was short and he got walloped once again. From there on out he struggled back at Triple-A, and what he contributes from this here crossroads is anybody's guess.

| YEAR | TEAM | LVL | AGE | WHIP | ERA | DRA | WARP | MPH | FB% | WHF | CSP |
|---|---|---|---|---|---|---|---|---|---|---|---|
| 2016 | ABQ | AAA | 23 | 1.36 | 4.02 | 3.96 | 1.9 | | | | |
| 2016 | COL | MLB | 23 | 1.72 | 4.88 | 7.05 | -0.6 | 96.8 | 58.7 | 8.2 | 47.3 |
| 2017 | ABQ | AAA | 24 | 1.27 | 4.71 | 4.57 | 0.6 | | | | |
| 2017 | COL | MLB | 24 | 1.47 | 5.89 | 6.08 | -0.6 | 96.5 | 67 | 8.9 | 50.7 |
| 2018 | COL | MLB | 25 | 2.54 | 9.35 | 7.23 | -0.2 | 94.7 | 53.9 | 8.9 | 42.8 |
| 2018 | ABQ | AAA | 25 | 1.44 | 4.94 | 4.13 | 1.7 | | | | |
| *2019* | *COL* | *MLB* | *26* | *1.40* | *4.30* | *4.48* | *0.4* | *96.0* | *65.3* | *8.9* | *47.4* |

*Jeff Hoffman, continued*

## Pitch Shape vs LHH

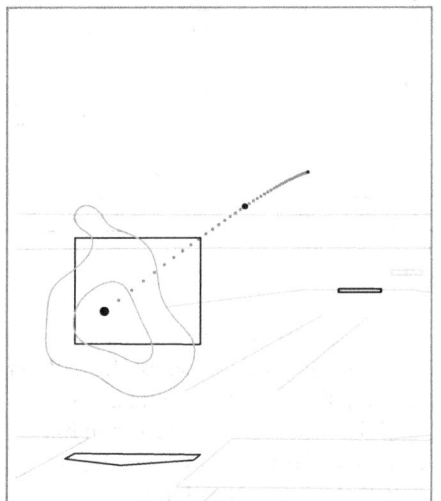

## Pitch Shape vs RHH

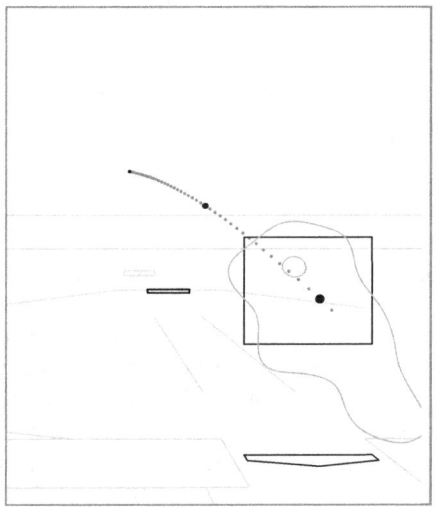

| Type | Frequency | Velocity | H Movement | V Movement |
|---|---|---|---|---|
| ● Fastball | 53.9% | 93.1 [102] | -7.6 [96] | -14.3 [105] |
| ☐ Sinker | | | | |
| + Cutter | | | | |
| ▲ Changeup | 12.8% | 86.9 [106] | -11.4 [100] | -23.1 [113] |
| × Splitter | | | | |
| ▽ Slider | 22.2% | 86.3 [108] | 2.7 [91] | -26.8 [118] |
| ◇ Curveball | 11.1% | 76.7 [94] | 8.7 [104] | -52.9 [89] |
| ⊕ Slow Curveball | | | | |
| ✱ Knuckleball | | | | |
| ▼ Screwball | | | | |

## German Marquez   RHP
Born: 02/22/95   Age: 24   Bats: R   Throws: R
Height: 6'1"   Weight: 185   Origin: International Free Agent, 2011

| YEAR | TEAM | LVL | AGE | W | L | SV | G | GS | IP | H | HR | BB/9 | K/9 | K | GB% | BABIP |
|---|---|---|---|---|---|---|---|---|---|---|---|---|---|---|---|---|
| 2016 | NBR | AAX | 21 | 9 | 6 | 0 | 21 | 21 | 135$^2$ | 124 | 9 | 2.2 | 8.4 | 126 | 48% | .304 |
| 2016 | ABQ | AAA | 21 | 2 | 0 | 0 | 5 | 5 | 31 | 30 | 5 | 1.7 | 8.4 | 29 | 45% | .298 |
| 2016 | COL | MLB | 21 | 1 | 1 | 0 | 6 | 3 | 20$^2$ | 28 | 2 | 2.6 | 6.5 | 15 | 55% | .361 |
| 2017 | ABQ | AAA | 22 | 0 | 0 | 0 | 3 | 2 | 10 | 8 | 2 | 0.0 | 16.2 | 18 | 53% | .353 |
| 2017 | COL | MLB | 22 | 11 | 7 | 0 | 29 | 29 | 162 | 174 | 25 | 2.7 | 8.2 | 147 | 47% | .316 |
| 2018 | COL | MLB | 23 | 14 | 11 | 0 | 33 | 33 | 196 | 179 | 24 | 2.6 | 10.6 | 230 | 48% | .312 |
| *2019* | *COL* | *MLB* | *24* | *11* | *7* | *0* | *28* | *28* | *159* | *144* | *16* | *2.7* | *10.0* | *177* | *46%* | *.303* |

Breakout: 27%   Improve: 67%   Collapse: 9%   Attrition: 14%   MLB: 97%
Comparables: Mike Minor, Drew Smyly, Matt Garza

It's weird to talk about the top of Colorado's rotation in glowing terms, but Marquez forced the issue after a stellar sophomore season. The evolution of his slider added a third lethal weapon to his arsenal, and with two well above-average spinners now in tow he left a trail of right-handed devastation in his wake. Lefties continued to see him pretty well, and if one were to pick non-Coors nits his lack of a reliable out pitch against the fairer-handed remains a heel fit for Achilles. The weakness wasn't nearly enough to derail one of the truly magnificent breakouts of 2018, however, and he even managed to offset his run prevention deficits with a Silver-Slugging effort at the dish. Still a year removed from arbitration eligibility, he'll enter the season as one of the most coveted assets in town.

| YEAR | TEAM | LVL | AGE | WHIP | ERA | DRA | WARP | MPH | FB% | WHF | CSP |
|---|---|---|---|---|---|---|---|---|---|---|---|
| 2016 | NBR | AAX | 21 | 1.16 | 2.85 | | | | | | |
| 2016 | ABQ | AAA | 21 | 1.16 | 4.35 | 4.18 | 0.4 | | | | |
| 2016 | COL | MLB | 21 | 1.65 | 5.23 | 5.71 | -0.1 | 96.8 | 62.6 | 9.8 | 54.6 |
| 2017 | ABQ | AAA | 22 | 0.80 | 2.70 | 2.80 | 0.3 | | | | |
| 2017 | COL | MLB | 22 | 1.38 | 4.39 | 5.08 | 0.9 | 97.5 | 65.5 | 10 | 53.7 |
| 2018 | COL | MLB | 23 | 1.20 | 3.77 | 3.23 | 4.7 | 97.5 | 54.9 | 13.4 | 49.9 |
| *2019* | *COL* | *MLB* | *24* | *1.21* | *3.28* | *3.41* | *3.1* | *97.3* | *61.1* | *12.3* | *53.9* |

*German Marquez, continued*

## Pitch Shape vs LHH

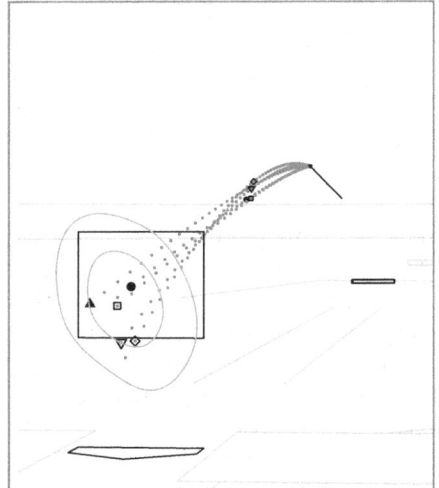

## Pitch Shape vs RHH

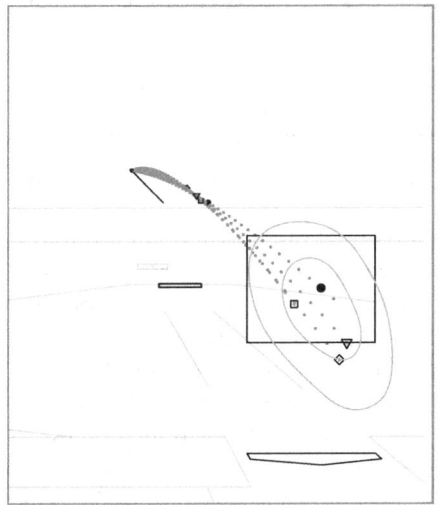

| Type | Frequency | Velocity | H Movement | V Movement |
|---|---|---|---|---|
| ● Fastball | 46.1% | 95.7 [110] | -5.2 [107] | -13.9 [106] |
| □ Sinker | 8.8% | 94.6 [111] | -11.6 [108] | -19.5 [103] |
| + Cutter | | | | |
| ▲ Changeup | 6.6% | 86.2 [103] | -9.8 [108] | -24.5 [108] |
| × Splitter | | | | |
| ▽ Slider | 18.2% | 85.7 [106] | 2.1 [88] | -32.2 [102] |
| ◇ Curveball | 20.2% | 82.1 [114] | 5.4 [90] | -42.6 [112] |
| ⊕ Slow Curveball | | | | |
| ✳ Knuckleball | | | | |
| ▼ Screwball | | | | |

## Jake McGee  LHP

Born: 08/06/86  Age: 32  Bats: L  Throws: L
Height: 6'3"  Weight: 230  Origin: Round 5, 2004 Draft (#135 overall)

| YEAR | TEAM | LVL | AGE | W | L | SV | G | GS | IP | H | HR | BB/9 | K/9 | K | GB% | BABIP |
|---|---|---|---|---|---|---|---|---|---|---|---|---|---|---|---|---|
| 2016 | COL | MLB | 29 | 2 | 3 | 15 | 57 | 0 | $45^2$ | 56 | 9 | 3.2 | 7.5 | 38 | 41% | .338 |
| 2017 | COL | MLB | 30 | 0 | 2 | 3 | 62 | 0 | $57^1$ | 47 | 4 | 2.5 | 9.1 | 58 | 40% | .287 |
| 2018 | COL | MLB | 31 | 2 | 4 | 1 | 61 | 0 | $51^1$ | 59 | 10 | 2.8 | 8.2 | 47 | 42% | .322 |
| 2019 | COL | MLB | 32 | 2 | 3 | 0 | 51 | 0 | 53 | 56 | 8 | 3.4 | 7.9 | 47 | 41% | .302 |

Breakout: 21%   Improve: 38%   Collapse: 30%   Attrition: 7%   MLB: 93%
Comparables: Joakim Soria, Rafael Betancourt, Darren O'Day

Here's the thing about being a one-pitch reliever: if that pitch ain't working, you won't be for much longer, either. There is of course a caveat, as that calculus changes a bit when you've just put pen to paper and guaranteed yourself $27 million. But a season removed from salvaging his standing and earning that deal, McGee once again took a wander down the wrong block. His velocity crept down a tick, but of greater concern was the speed at which his pitched balls came screaming back in the other direction. His once-formidable heater increasingly looks miscast in the lift-and-launch era, as hitters routinely pummeled the pitch down in the zone en route to a 91st percentile exit velocity. A late-season flirtation with more sliders did little to stem the tide, and he'll continue his search for an adjustment that'll stick in 2019.

| YEAR | TEAM | LVL | AGE | WHIP | ERA | DRA | WARP | MPH | FB% | WHF | CSP |
|---|---|---|---|---|---|---|---|---|---|---|---|
| 2016 | COL | MLB | 29 | 1.58 | 4.73 | 7.01 | -1.1 | 96.5 | 84.3 | 10.3 | 50 |
| 2017 | COL | MLB | 30 | 1.10 | 3.61 | 4.26 | 0.6 | 97.2 | 93.4 | 10.2 | 51.9 |
| 2018 | COL | MLB | 31 | 1.46 | 6.49 | 6.15 | -0.7 | 96.2 | 86.3 | 11.1 | 53.2 |
| 2019 | COL | MLB | 32 | 1.44 | 4.83 | 4.82 | 0.0 | 95.7 | 87.5 | 10.5 | 51.5 |

*Jake McGee, continued*

### Pitch Shape vs LHH

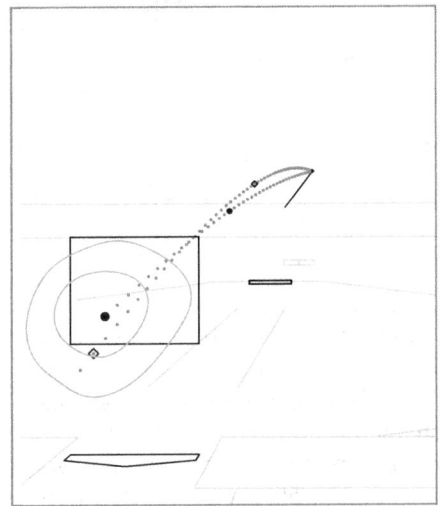

### Pitch Shape vs RHH

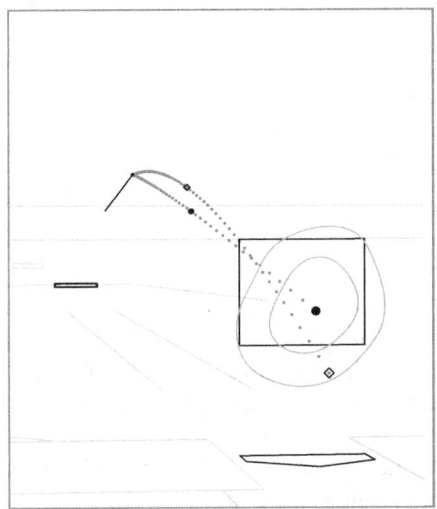

| Type | Frequency | Velocity | H Movement | V Movement |
|---|---|---|---|---|
| ● Fastball | 86.3% | 94.2 [105] | 8.6 [91] | -14 [106] |
| ☐ Sinker | | | | |
| + Cutter | | | | |
| ▲ Changeup | | | | |
| ✕ Splitter | | | | |
| ▽ Slider | 5.1% | 82.4 [91] | -1.9 [87] | -33.6 [98] |
| ◇ Curveball | 8.6% | 78.3 [100] | -3.1 [80] | -44.9 [107] |
| ⊕ Slow Curveball | | | | |
| ✱ Knuckleball | | | | |
| ▼ Screwball | | | | |

Colorado Rockies 2019

## Harrison Musgrave  LHP
Born: 03/03/92   Age: 27   Bats: L   Throws: L
Height: 6'1"   Weight: 205   Origin: Round 8, 2014 Draft (#233 overall)

| YEAR | TEAM | LVL | AGE | W | L | SV | G | GS | IP | H | HR | BB/9 | K/9 | K | GB% | BABIP |
|---|---|---|---|---|---|---|---|---|---|---|---|---|---|---|---|---|
| 2016 | NBR | AAX | 24 | 5 | 1 | 0 | 6 | 6 | 40$^1$ | 20 | 1 | 1.8 | 6.7 | 30 | 51% | .174 |
| 2016 | ABQ | AAA | 24 | 8 | 7 | 0 | 19 | 19 | 113 | 118 | 17 | 3.2 | 6.3 | 79 | 43% | .292 |
| 2017 | ABQ | AAA | 25 | 3 | 1 | 0 | 12 | 12 | 54$^1$ | 64 | 10 | 4.3 | 6.5 | 39 | 41% | .318 |
| 2018 | ABQ | AAA | 26 | 0 | 1 | 0 | 8 | 3 | 16$^2$ | 23 | 2 | 3.2 | 9.7 | 18 | 44% | .404 |
| 2018 | COL | MLB | 26 | 2 | 3 | 0 | 35 | 0 | 44$^2$ | 36 | 7 | 4.4 | 6.4 | 32 | 40% | .236 |
| 2019 | COL | MLB | 27 | 1 | 2 | 0 | 31 | 0 | 32$^1$ | 31 | 5 | 3.9 | 7.7 | 28 | 42% | .290 |

Breakout: 4%   Improve: 12%   Collapse: 21%   Attrition: 28%   MLB: 47%
Comparables: Joe Biagini, Anthony Ranaudo, Chris Stratton

Harrison Musgrave, pitcher, made the majors in 2018 and was about as interesting to watch as Harrison Musgrave, guest lecturer on the Teapot Dome Scandal. Back around the time Colorado drafted him in the round where teams draft polished Big 12 pitchers with limited upside, he projected for fringy big-league utility on the back of an average-ish fastball and a sure, okay, fine changeup from the left side. Well, here we are a handful of years later and you can chalk one up for the scouts. The cambio actually played a bit better than advertised in the bigs, but right-handers ruthlessly pummeled his spin and speed. There are probably still some useful days ahead of him—he *is* left-handed, after all—although that's what they used to say about ol' Warren G. Harding, too.

| YEAR | TEAM | LVL | AGE | WHIP | ERA | DRA | WARP | MPH | FB% | WHF | CSP |
|---|---|---|---|---|---|---|---|---|---|---|---|
| 2016 | NBR | AAX | 24 | 0.69 | 1.79 | | | | | | |
| 2016 | ABQ | AAA | 24 | 1.40 | 4.30 | 4.24 | 1.4 | | | | |
| 2017 | ABQ | AAA | 25 | 1.66 | 6.79 | 4.79 | 0.5 | | | | |
| 2018 | ABQ | AAA | 26 | 1.74 | 5.40 | 3.61 | 0.3 | | | | |
| 2018 | COL | MLB | 26 | 1.30 | 4.63 | 6.70 | -0.9 | 92.9 | 59.5 | 10.7 | 42.7 |
| 2019 | COL | MLB | 27 | 1.41 | 5.01 | 4.96 | -0.1 | 92.4 | 60.2 | 10.9 | 43.2 |

**Harrison Musgrave, continued**

### Pitch Shape vs LHH

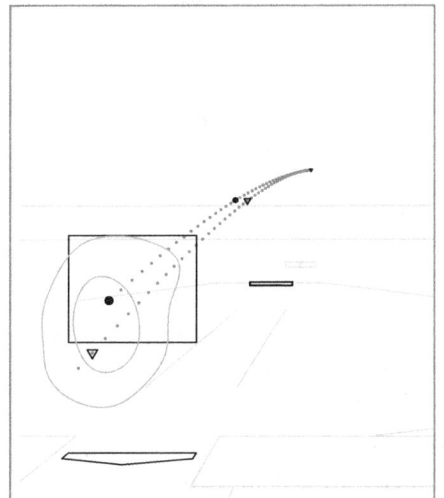

### Pitch Shape vs RHH

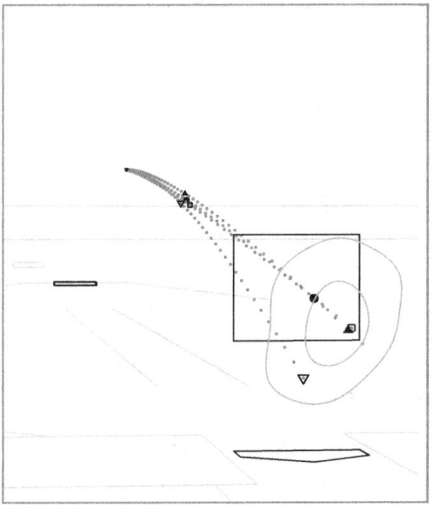

| Type | Frequency | Velocity | H Movement | V Movement |
|---|---|---|---|---|
| ● Fastball | 46.8% | 91.4 [96] | 5.9 [104] | -16.9 [96] |
| ☐ Sinker | 12.7% | 91.1 [93] | 11.7 [108] | -18.2 [107] |
| + Cutter | | | | |
| ▲ Changeup | 16.3% | 81.8 [86] | 7.1 [122] | -27.2 [101] |
| ✕ Splitter | | | | |
| ▽ Slider | 24.0% | 83.3 [95] | -3.9 [96] | -29 [112] |
| ◇ Curveball | 0.1% | 71 [72] | -8.1 [101] | -50.1 [95] |
| ⊕ Slow Curveball | | | | |
| ✳ Knuckleball | | | | |
| ▼ Screwball | | | | |

Colorado Rockies 2019

### Scott Oberg   RHP
Born: 03/13/90   Age: 29   Bats: R   Throws: R
Height: 6'2"   Weight: 205   Origin: Round 15, 2012 Draft (#468 overall)

| YEAR | TEAM | LVL | AGE | W | L | SV | G | GS | IP | H | HR | BB/9 | K/9 | K | GB% | BABIP |
|---|---|---|---|---|---|---|---|---|---|---|---|---|---|---|---|---|
| 2016 | ABQ | AAA | 26 | 1 | 0 | 9 | 27 | 0 | $29^2$ | 16 | 1 | 3.3 | 10.9 | 36 | 54% | .234 |
| 2016 | COL | MLB | 26 | 1 | 1 | 1 | 24 | 0 | 26 | 26 | 3 | 3.8 | 6.9 | 20 | 56% | .295 |
| 2017 | COL | MLB | 27 | 0 | 1 | 0 | 66 | 0 | $58^1$ | 70 | 4 | 3.7 | 8.5 | 55 | 58% | .367 |
| 2018 | ABQ | AAA | 28 | 1 | 0 | 3 | 13 | 0 | $15^1$ | 14 | 1 | 1.2 | 8.2 | 14 | 62% | .333 |
| 2018 | COL | MLB | 28 | 8 | 1 | 0 | 56 | 0 | $58^2$ | 45 | 4 | 1.8 | 8.7 | 57 | 58% | .270 |
| 2019 | COL | MLB | 29 | 2 | 3 | 0 | 51 | 0 | 53 | 51 | 6 | 3.5 | 8.7 | 52 | 52% | .302 |

Breakout: 28%   Improve: 46%   Collapse: 28%   Attrition: 21%   MLB: 92%
Comparables: Ryan Pressly, Jared Burton, Hunter Strickland

Step 1: sit 96 off an arm-strength delivery.
Step 2: start missing entirely or at least getting under the barrel of like four out of every five swinging bats with a high-80s, two-plane slider.
Step 3: stop throwing basically every other pitch.

So went the formula for Oberg's ascension from solid-if-unspectacular middle man to frothy highest-leverage October arm. By the time the Brewers cancelled Rocktober the right-hander was among the last reliable men standing in a ravaged bullpen, and even his uppins came in the decisive game. Despite the salty final bite, it was a dynamic rise for the former 15th-rounder, who survived a late-April meltdown and demotion to return a month later and yield five runs over the next nigh-on four months. As he'll arbitrate his first contract this winter, he should remain cheap enough for the Rockies to rely on for the next couple years.

| YEAR | TEAM | LVL | AGE | WHIP | ERA | DRA | WARP | MPH | FB% | WHF | CSP |
|---|---|---|---|---|---|---|---|---|---|---|---|
| 2016 | ABQ | AAA | 26 | 0.91 | 2.43 | 2.59 | 0.8 | | | | |
| 2016 | COL | MLB | 26 | 1.42 | 5.19 | 5.34 | -0.1 | 97.2 | 60 | 10.7 | 47.6 |
| 2017 | COL | MLB | 27 | 1.61 | 4.94 | 4.89 | 0.2 | 98.1 | 56.4 | 12.2 | 50.5 |
| 2018 | ABQ | AAA | 28 | 1.04 | 1.76 | 3.94 | 0.2 | | | | |
| 2018 | COL | MLB | 28 | 0.97 | 2.45 | 3.49 | 1.0 | 97.0 | 55.1 | 14.7 | 48.1 |
| 2019 | COL | MLB | 29 | 1.35 | 3.79 | 4.02 | 0.5 | 96.8 | 56.3 | 13.2 | 48.8 |

**Scott Oberg, continued**

### Pitch Shape vs LHH

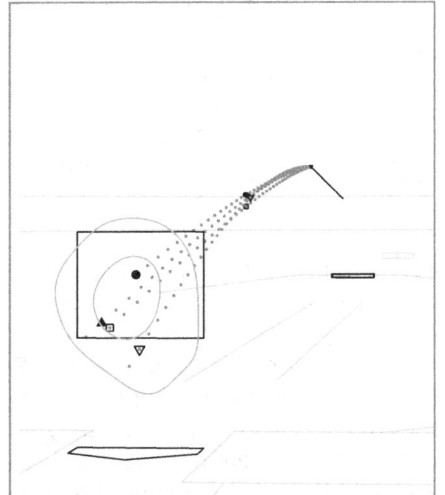

### Pitch Shape vs RHH

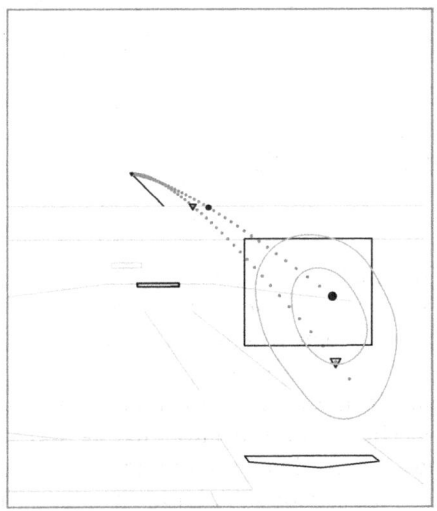

| Type | Frequency | Velocity | H Movement | V Movement |
|---|---|---|---|---|
| ● Fastball | 48.8% | 96 [111] | -1.4 [125] | -14.1 [105] |
| □ Sinker | 6.3% | 94.6 [111] | -8.9 [130] | -20.1 [101] |
| + Cutter | | | | |
| ▲ Changeup | 7.4% | 89.2 [115] | -10.9 [102] | -25.5 [106] |
| × Splitter | | | | |
| ▽ Slider | 37.4% | 87.3 [112] | 5.1 [101] | -32.3 [102] |
| ◇ Curveball | 0.1% | 76.6 [93] | 11.3 [115] | -49.9 [96] |
| ⊕ Slow Curveball | | | | |
| ✱ Knuckleball | | | | |
| ▼ Screwball | | | | |

## Seung Hwan Oh  RHP

Born: 07/15/82   Age: 36   Bats: R   Throws: R
Height: 5'10"   Weight: 205   Origin: International Free Agent, 2016

| YEAR | TEAM | LVL | AGE | W | L | SV | G | GS | IP | H | HR | BB/9 | K/9 | K | GB% | BABIP |
|---|---|---|---|---|---|---|---|---|---|---|---|---|---|---|---|---|
| 2016 | SLN | MLB | 33 | 6 | 3 | 19 | 76 | 0 | 79$^2$ | 55 | 5 | 2.0 | 11.6 | 103 | 40% | .270 |
| 2017 | SLN | MLB | 34 | 1 | 6 | 20 | 62 | 0 | 59$^1$ | 68 | 10 | 2.3 | 8.2 | 54 | 30% | .319 |
| 2018 | TOR | MLB | 35 | 4 | 3 | 2 | 48 | 0 | 47 | 37 | 5 | 1.9 | 10.5 | 55 | 31% | .276 |
| 2018 | COL | MLB | 35 | 2 | 0 | 1 | 25 | 0 | 21$^1$ | 15 | 3 | 3.0 | 10.1 | 24 | 30% | .240 |
| 2019 | COL | MLB | 36 | 2 | 3 | 3 | 51 | 0 | 53 | 54 | 9 | 3.2 | 9.6 | 57 | 35% | .302 |

Breakout: 27%   Improve: 38%   Collapse: 28%   Attrition: 6%   MLB: 79%
Comparables: Jim Brewer, Arthur Rhodes, Tom Gordon

The Final Boss morphed into more of a Middle Innings Boss in 2018, a Bald Bull for the modern era. His charge still hit hard, and he blew his four-seamer by hitters at a near-elite clip despite the pitch creaking down to 92. It was a nice return to form after his struggles during a second season in St. Louis, even if DRA wasn't convinced on the merits. The Rockies were, however, and imported him with his trusty translator Eugene Koo for the stretch run. They got what they bought, as Oh manufactured a bunch of outs at a time when that wasn't the cool thing to do in Colorado's bullpen. The club holds a no-brainer option on a full season of his services, and the greatest Korean reliever in the game's history should have opportunity to pitch for as long as he can and will.

| YEAR | TEAM | LVL | AGE | WHIP | ERA | DRA | WARP | MPH | FB% | WHF | CSP |
|---|---|---|---|---|---|---|---|---|---|---|---|
| 2016 | SLN | MLB | 33 | 0.92 | 1.92 | 2.24 | 2.5 | 95.7 | 60.7 | 18.7 | 45.8 |
| 2017 | SLN | MLB | 34 | 1.40 | 4.10 | 5.70 | -0.4 | 94.4 | 61.9 | 14.7 | 49.9 |
| 2018 | TOR | MLB | 35 | 1.00 | 2.68 | 4.31 | 0.3 | 93.1 | 57.5 | 15.2 | 46.6 |
| 2018 | COL | MLB | 35 | 1.03 | 2.53 | 4.81 | 0.0 | 93.2 | 43.6 | 17.6 | 42.9 |
| 2019 | COL | MLB | 36 | 1.36 | 4.52 | 4.59 | 0.1 | 92.9 | 56.7 | 16 | 46 |

*Seung Hwan Oh, continued*

## Pitch Shape vs LHH

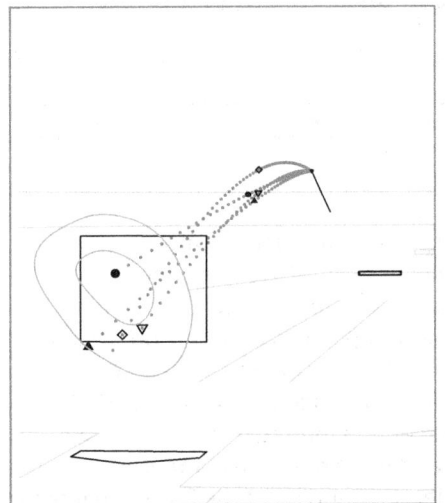

## Pitch Shape vs RHH

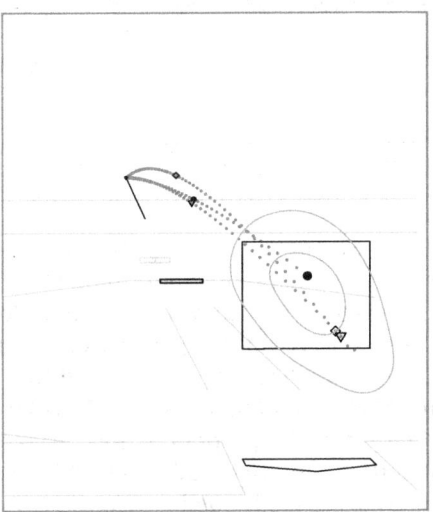

| Type | Frequency | Velocity | H Movement | V Movement |
|---|---|---|---|---|
| ● Fastball | 51.6% | 92.1 [99] | -4.9 [108] | -13.8 [106] |
| ☐ Sinker | 1.7% | 91.6 [96] | -13.4 [94] | -18 [108] |
| + Cutter | | | | |
| ▲ Changeup | 7.8% | 84.3 [96] | -11.3 [100] | -25.7 [105] |
| ✕ Splitter | | | | |
| ▽ Slider | 31.0% | 84.5 [100] | 3 [92] | -29 [112] |
| ◇ Curveball | 7.8% | 74.8 [87] | 6 [92] | -51.7 [92] |
| ⊕ Slow Curveball | | | | |
| ✱ Knuckleball | | | | |
| ▼ Screwball | | | | |

## Chris Rusin   LHP

Born: 10/22/86   Age: 32   Bats: L   Throws: L
Height: 6'2"   Weight: 195   Origin: Round 4, 2009 Draft (#140 overall)

| YEAR | TEAM | LVL | AGE | W | L | SV | G | GS | IP | H | HR | BB/9 | K/9 | K | GB% | BABIP |
|---|---|---|---|---|---|---|---|---|---|---|---|---|---|---|---|---|
| 2016 | COL | MLB | 29 | 3 | 5 | 0 | 29 | 7 | 84$^1$ | 82 | 5 | 2.5 | 7.4 | 69 | 61% | .308 |
| 2017 | COL | MLB | 30 | 5 | 1 | 2 | 60 | 0 | 85 | 75 | 9 | 2.0 | 7.5 | 71 | 60% | .277 |
| 2018 | COL | MLB | 31 | 2 | 3 | 0 | 49 | 0 | 54$^2$ | 56 | 7 | 4.3 | 7.7 | 47 | 57% | .308 |
| 2019 | COL | MLB | 32 | 2 | 2 | 0 | 41 | 0 | 43 | 43 | 4 | 3.6 | 7.8 | 37 | 54% | .303 |

Breakout: 18%   Improve: 38%   Collapse: 19%   Attrition: 14%   MLB: 75%
Comparables: Scott Downs, Casey Fossum, Dillon Gee

Folks, we might as well call the Rockies' bullpen "American democracy" because a Rusin sure undermined the hell out of it in 2018. It's generally not a great sign when a player's high point for an entire season occurs in March, but there he was, inheriting a bases-loaded, no-out jam in a tight one on Opening Day. He got that left-left punchout they were looking for, the next-best-thing pop fly followed and then just the kind of harmless inning-ending rollover that affords time for proper histrionics heading off the mound. His reward? Two inherited runs on his tab the next inning and four consecutive months of injured, ineffective ugliness for his trouble. He found it in time for the real show, logging scoreless appearances in each one of the club's postseason games. It wasn't exactly a happy ending, but there was surely a satisfied nod to be seen. There's no hope for lifting the sanctions on him starting games, but lefties don't handle his sinker especially well and he's still cheap—both traits that tend to bode well for longevity.

| YEAR | TEAM | LVL | AGE | WHIP | ERA | DRA | WARP | MPH | FB% | WHF | CSP |
|---|---|---|---|---|---|---|---|---|---|---|---|
| 2016 | COL | MLB | 29 | 1.25 | 3.74 | 4.39 | 0.7 | 91.7 | 43.3 | 10.2 | 46.5 |
| 2017 | COL | MLB | 30 | 1.11 | 2.65 | 3.49 | 1.6 | 92.6 | 43.1 | 13.2 | 48.7 |
| 2018 | COL | MLB | 31 | 1.50 | 6.09 | 5.62 | -0.4 | 91.4 | 50.7 | 10 | 47.5 |
| 2019 | COL | MLB | 32 | 1.41 | 3.97 | 4.16 | 0.3 | 91.0 | 45.3 | 11.2 | 47.2 |

**Chris Rusin, continued**

### Pitch Shape vs LHH

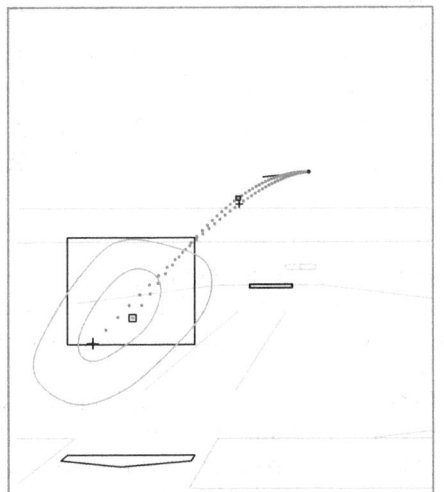

### Pitch Shape vs RHH

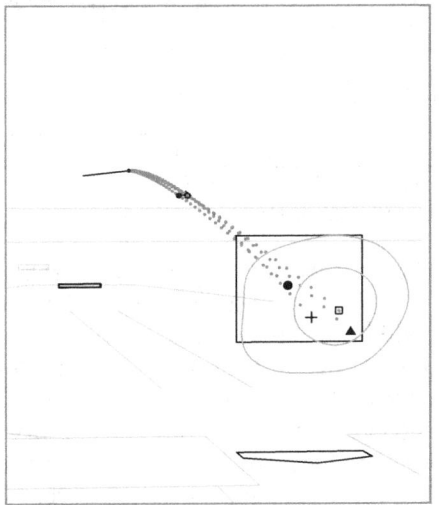

| Type | Frequency | Velocity | H Movement | V Movement |
|---|---|---|---|---|
| ● Fastball | 7.8% | 91.4 [96] | 5.7 [105] | -17 [96] |
| □ Sinker | 43.0% | 90.5 [90] | 12.4 [102] | -23.9 [89] |
| + Cutter | 27.9% | 87.9 [95] | -0.7 [93] | -25.1 [95] |
| ▲ Changeup | 17.0% | 84.2 [96] | 11.3 [100] | -28.9 [95] |
| × Splitter | | | | |
| ▽ Slider | 3.0% | 81.8 [88] | -3.7 [95] | -36.6 [89] |
| ◇ Curveball | 1.4% | 81.2 [110] | -3.5 [82] | -38.6 [121] |
| ⊕ Slow Curveball | | | | |
| ✳ Knuckleball | | | | |
| ▼ Screwball | | | | |

## Antonio Senzatela  RHP

Born: 01/21/95   Age: 24   Bats: R   Throws: R
Height: 6'1"   Weight: 180   Origin: International Free Agent, 2011

| YEAR | TEAM | LVL | AGE | W | L | SV | G | GS | IP | H | HR | BB/9 | K/9 | K | GB% | BABIP |
|---|---|---|---|---|---|---|---|---|---|---|---|---|---|---|---|---|
| 2016 | NBR | AAX | 21 | 4 | 1 | 0 | 7 | 7 | 34$^2$ | 27 | 1 | 2.3 | 7.0 | 27 | 44% | .265 |
| 2017 | COL | MLB | 22 | 10 | 5 | 0 | 36 | 20 | 134$^2$ | 128 | 18 | 3.1 | 6.8 | 102 | 50% | .280 |
| 2018 | ABQ | AAA | 23 | 3 | 1 | 0 | 8 | 8 | 37$^2$ | 29 | 1 | 2.9 | 10.0 | 42 | 48% | .298 |
| 2018 | COL | MLB | 23 | 6 | 6 | 0 | 23 | 13 | 90$^1$ | 94 | 10 | 3.0 | 6.9 | 69 | 47% | .302 |
| 2019 | COL | MLB | 24 | 8 | 7 | 0 | 39 | 19 | 122$^1$ | 121 | 15 | 3.1 | 7.5 | 101 | 45% | .295 |

Breakout: 20%   Improve: 47%   Collapse: 21%   Attrition: 20%   MLB: 92%
Comparables: Jeremy Sowers, Jarrod Parker, Zach Duke

There's a certain responsibility that comes with being a not-enormous right-hander; certain assumptions to defy. Senzatela's up-and-over delivery helps his good fastball play better, but his career's path to date has been defined by a not-quite-successful quest to find things to throw with it. The slider's his strikeout pitch and a clear number two on his depth chart. But hitters slugged it like each and every one of 'em was Trevor Story last year. His change has always been a little too firm, and fly balls are dangerous balls (yes, especially so in Coors Field). The curve got decent results last year, but again, that thing about fly balls in Coors. His swing role on the cheap is a valuable one for every big-league team, and with arbitration still two years away it's a role that should suit him for the foreseeable future.

| YEAR | TEAM | LVL | AGE | WHIP | ERA | DRA | WARP | MPH | FB% | WHF | CSP |
|---|---|---|---|---|---|---|---|---|---|---|---|
| 2016 | NBR | AAX | 21 | 1.04 | 1.82 | | | | | | |
| 2017 | COL | MLB | 22 | 1.30 | 4.68 | 4.63 | 1.3 | 96.9 | 71.8 | 7.6 | 52.2 |
| 2018 | ABQ | AAA | 23 | 1.09 | 2.15 | 4.27 | 0.5 | | | | |
| 2018 | COL | MLB | 23 | 1.37 | 4.38 | 5.10 | 0.1 | 96.0 | 64.1 | 8.9 | 47.5 |
| 2019 | COL | MLB | 24 | 1.34 | 4.27 | 4.44 | 0.8 | 96.3 | 70.3 | 8.5 | 51.1 |

*Antonio Senzatela, continued*

## Pitch Shape vs LHH

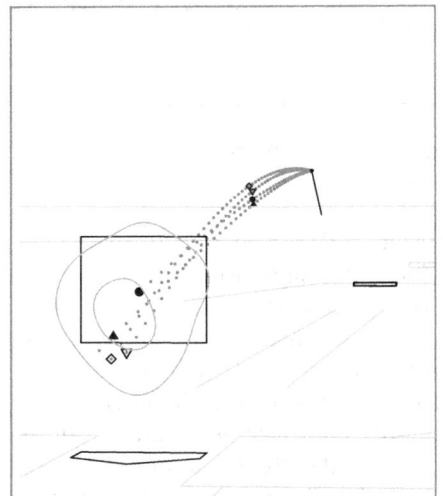

## Pitch Shape vs RHH

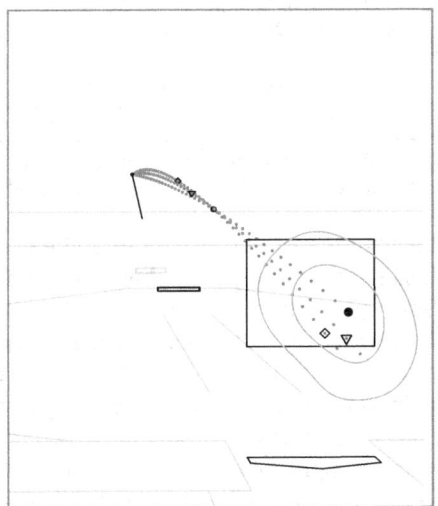

| Type | Frequency | Velocity | H Movement | V Movement |
|---|---|---|---|---|
| ● Fastball | 64.1% | 94.2 [105] | -3.7 [114] | -16.4 [98] |
| ☐ Sinker | | | | |
| + Cutter | | | | |
| ▲ Changeup | 8.7% | 87.1 [107] | -8 [117] | -23.6 [111] |
| ✕ Splitter | | | | |
| ▽ Slider | 18.8% | 83.4 [95] | 5.7 [104] | -35.8 [92] |
| ◇ Curveball | 8.4% | 78.8 [101] | 8.2 [102] | -43.3 [111] |
| ⊕ Slow Curveball | | | | |
| ✱ Knuckleball | | | | |
| ▼ Screwball | | | | |

## Bryan Shaw  RHP
Born: 11/08/87  Age: 31  Bats: B  Throws: R
Height: 6'1"  Weight: 220  Origin: Round 2, 2008 Draft (#73 overall)

| YEAR | TEAM | LVL | AGE | W | L | SV | G | GS | IP | H | HR | BB/9 | K/9 | K | GB% | BABIP |
|---|---|---|---|---|---|---|---|---|---|---|---|---|---|---|---|---|
| 2016 | CLE | MLB | 28 | 2 | 5 | 1 | 75 | 0 | 66² | 56 | 8 | 3.8 | 9.3 | 69 | 56% | .284 |
| 2017 | CLE | MLB | 29 | 4 | 6 | 3 | 79 | 0 | 76² | 71 | 5 | 2.6 | 8.6 | 73 | 57% | .311 |
| 2018 | COL | MLB | 30 | 4 | 6 | 0 | 61 | 0 | 54² | 70 | 9 | 4.6 | 8.9 | 54 | 49% | .370 |
| 2019 | COL | MLB | 31 | 2 | 3 | 0 | 51 | 0 | 53 | 54 | 7 | 4.0 | 8.1 | 48 | 51% | .303 |

Breakout: 31%  Improve: 54%  Collapse: 19%  Attrition: 10%  MLB: 90%
Comparables: Mike MacDougal, Bob Locker, Rafael Perez

Paying for past performance can be expensive, and sure enough, fresh off inking his first big-money deal Shaw looked anything but. Right from the jump in Spring Training he rather resembled the weathered part of a guy who led all of baseball in appearances over the previous five seasons. He never did get quite right in the season's first half, with a snowball of mid-season ineffectiveness culminating in the iron man getting put on ice for the first time in his career, a calf issue ostensibly to blame. The performance improved upon return, but the warning signs never stopped flashing; his patented cutter left a couple ticks of velocity in the trainer's room, he worked in back-to-back games but once more and Bud Black hailed his way just four times in September before leaving him off the playoff roster entirely. Like most of his bullpen-mates he'll look to hit the reset button this winter.

| YEAR | TEAM | LVL | AGE | WHIP | ERA | DRA | WARP | MPH | FB% | WHF | CSP |
|---|---|---|---|---|---|---|---|---|---|---|---|
| 2016 | CLE | MLB | 28 | 1.26 | 3.24 | 3.49 | 1.1 | 95.9 | 81.4 | 12.9 | 47.5 |
| 2017 | CLE | MLB | 29 | 1.21 | 3.52 | 2.73 | 2.1 | 96.5 | 88.2 | 13.1 | 48.4 |
| 2018 | COL | MLB | 30 | 1.79 | 5.93 | 4.07 | 0.5 | 95.9 | 84.8 | 12.5 | 43.8 |
| 2019 | COL | MLB | 31 | 1.46 | 4.43 | 4.53 | 0.2 | 95.3 | 84.7 | 12.8 | 46 |

*Bryan Shaw, continued*

## Pitch Shape vs LHH

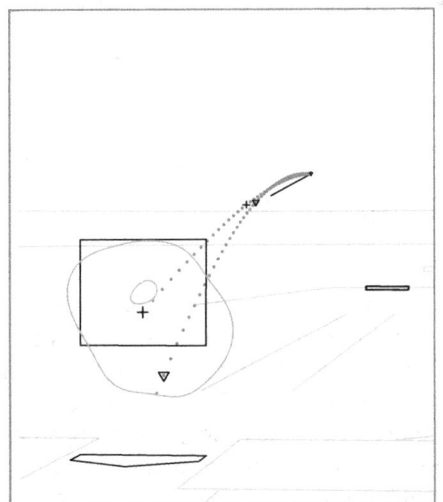

## Pitch Shape vs RHH

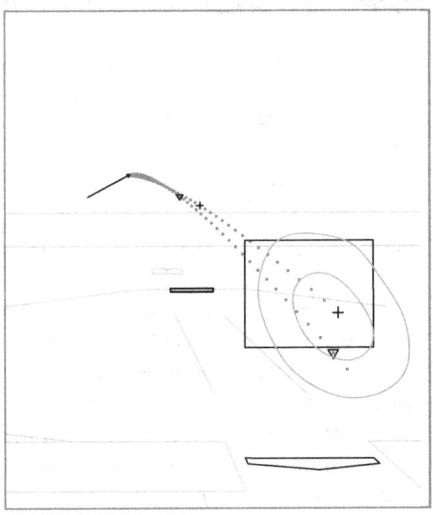

| Type | Frequency | Velocity | H Movement | V Movement |
|---|---|---|---|---|
| ● Fastball | | | | |
| ☐ Sinker | 0.5% | 94.6 [111] | -5.8 [156] | -21.3 [97] |
| + Cutter | 84.3% | 93.9 [131] | 4.2 [114] | -21 [111] |
| ▲ Changeup | 0.1% | 84 [95] | -8.2 [116] | -27.9 [98] |
| ✕ Splitter | | | | |
| ▽ Slider | 15.1% | 83.6 [96] | 12.2 [132] | -38.4 [84] |
| ◇ Curveball | | | | |
| ✜ Slow Curveball | | | | |
| ✳ Knuckleball | | | | |
| ▼ Screwball | | | | |

Rockies Player Analysis - 75

## Garrett Hampson  MI

Born: 10/10/94   Age: 24   Bats: R   Throws: R
Height: 5'11"   Weight: 185   Origin: Round 3, 2016 Draft (#81 overall)

| YEAR | TEAM | LVL | AGE | PA | R | 2B | 3B | HR | RBI | BB | K | SB | CS | AVG/OBP/SLG |
|---|---|---|---|---|---|---|---|---|---|---|---|---|---|---|
| 2016 | BOI | A- | 21 | 312 | 43 | 14 | 8 | 2 | 44 | 48 | 56 | 36 | 4 | .301/.404/.441 |
| 2017 | LNC | A+ | 22 | 603 | 113 | 24 | 12 | 8 | 70 | 56 | 77 | 51 | 14 | .326/.387/.462 |
| 2018 | HFD | AA | 23 | 172 | 28 | 8 | 2 | 4 | 15 | 21 | 17 | 19 | 1 | .304/.391/.466 |
| 2018 | ABQ | AAA | 23 | 332 | 53 | 17 | 4 | 6 | 25 | 30 | 58 | 17 | 4 | .314/.377/.459 |
| 2018 | COL | MLB | 23 | 48 | 3 | 3 | 1 | 0 | 4 | 7 | 12 | 2 | 0 | .275/.396/.400 |
| 2019 | COL | MLB | 24 | 368 | 46 | 16 | 4 | 10 | 41 | 29 | 73 | 18 | 3 | .267/.327/.429 |

Breakout: 9%   Improve: 23%   Collapse: 0%   Attrition: 23%   MLB: 38%
Comparables: Jose Pirela, Matt Antonelli, Tim Locastro

The High Plains stretch out and yawn across a huge swath of miles and tribes and states, over a mass of land that is vast in expanse and, for the purposes of its only resident big-league baseball club, elevation. The High Plains reside at an unusual height for plains, and a consequence of height on Earth is wind. Steady, consistent, flowing air, more robust in its bluster at some times, humming along unflinchingly from the west at most others. Hampson is going to fit right in. He grinds, he hums, he flows. He executes quality baseball plays over, and over, and over again. At every level he's stretched out, yawned, and played—up to and including a couple delicious cups of coffee last season. He hits, he runs, he defends well at multiple positions, and he gets every inch, every pebble, out of his game. DJ LeMahieu is going to walk out that door, Garrett Hampson is poised to walk in, and if history's any kind of a guide the winds will grumble on as the soundtrack to a most peaceful transfer of power.

| YEAR | TEAM | LVL | AGE | PA | DRC+ | VORP | BABIP | BRR | FRAA | WARP |
|---|---|---|---|---|---|---|---|---|---|---|
| 2016 | BOI | A- | 21 | 312 | 154 | 36.7 | .366 | 4.6 | SS(64): 8.2, 2B(1): -0.2 | 2.9 |
| 2017 | LNC | A+ | 22 | 603 | 130 | 41.6 | .364 | 7.5 | 2B(71): -0.4, SS(56): 7.3 | 3.9 |
| 2018 | HFD | AA | 23 | 172 | 136 | 18.7 | .323 | 3.5 | SS(18): 0.4, 2B(17): 1.7 | 1.6 |
| 2018 | ABQ | AAA | 23 | 332 | 110 | 16.8 | .372 | 0.9 | 2B(44): -0.1, SS(23): -2.3 | 1.1 |
| 2018 | COL | MLB | 23 | 48 | 81 | 3.5 | .393 | 1.1 | SS(8): 0.2, 2B(7): 0.6 | 0.2 |
| 2019 | COL | MLB | 24 | 368 | 90 | 11.7 | .311 | 2.7 | 2B 0, CF 0 | 1.2 |

## Sam Hilliard   RF

Born: 02/21/94   Age: 25   Bats: L   Throws: L
Height: 6'5"   Weight: 225   Origin: Round 15, 2015 Draft (#437 overall)

| YEAR | TEAM | LVL | AGE | PA | R | 2B | 3B | HR | RBI | BB | K | SB | CS | AVG/OBP/SLG |
|---|---|---|---|---|---|---|---|---|---|---|---|---|---|---|
| 2016 | ASH | A | 22 | 527 | 71 | 23 | 5 | 17 | 83 | 56 | 150 | 30 | 12 | .267/.348/.449 |
| 2017 | LNC | A+ | 23 | 597 | 95 | 23 | 7 | 21 | 92 | 50 | 154 | 37 | 17 | .300/.360/.487 |
| 2018 | HFD | AA | 24 | 484 | 58 | 22 | 3 | 9 | 40 | 41 | 151 | 23 | 14 | .262/.327/.389 |
| 2019 | COL | MLB | 25 | 251 | 27 | 8 | 1 | 7 | 26 | 15 | 87 | 8 | 4 | .206/.252/.340 |

Breakout: 1%   Improve: 4%   Collapse: 1%   Attrition: 6%   MLB: 7%
Comparables: Joey Butler, Jared Hoying, Brandon Barnes

A results-heavy effort at Lancaster led to wait-and-see verdicts for Hilliard last winter, and it was Double-A pitchers who went and did the seeing. Hilliard's lagging swing got shot full of holes by more advanced arms, particularly the left-handed kind. The impressive speed for his size didn't play any finer against better batteries, either. He offers some outfield versatility, but that can only take him so far, and it can get late early for former 15th rounders with big whiff issues who are repeating Double-A at 25. On the plus side, he remains a physical specimen, and his bat has flickered enough that he toppled Jordan Patterson from the 40-man this winter. At the very least he should invite strong-side platoon auditions for a couple more years, and there remains a chance for big-league value despite a rough introduction to the high minors.

| YEAR | TEAM | LVL | AGE | PA | DRC+ | VORP | BABIP | BRR | FRAA | WARP |
|---|---|---|---|---|---|---|---|---|---|---|
| 2016 | ASH | A | 22 | 527 | 115 | 20.3 | .357 | 2.2 | LF(62): 0.1, RF(56): -0.6 | 1.0 |
| 2017 | LNC | A+ | 23 | 597 | 122 | 25.2 | .384 | 3.9 | RF(85): 6.6, LF(30): 5.1 | 2.6 |
| 2018 | HFD | AA | 24 | 484 | 98 | 9.1 | .379 | 0.3 | RF(70): 3.5, LF(29): -1.8 | 0.3 |
| 2019 | COL | MLB | 25 | 251 | 56 | -5.8 | .286 | 0.2 | RF 0, LF 0 | -0.6 |

### Grant Lavigne  1B
Born: 08/27/99  Age: 19  Bats: L  Throws: R
Height: 6'4"  Weight: 220  Origin: Round 1, 2018 Draft (#42 overall)

| YEAR | TEAM | LVL | AGE | PA | R | 2B | 3B | HR | RBI | BB | K | SB | CS | AVG/OBP/SLG |
|---|---|---|---|---|---|---|---|---|---|---|---|---|---|---|
| 2018 | GJR | RK | 18 | 258 | 45 | 13 | 2 | 6 | 38 | 45 | 40 | 12 | 7 | .350/.477/.519 |
| 2019 | COL | MLB | 19 | 251 | 24 | 7 | 0 | 7 | 26 | 26 | 70 | 2 | 1 | .193/.275/.315 |

Breakout: 7%   Improve: 9%   Collapse: 0%   Attrition: 4%   MLB: 12%
Comparables: Franmil Reyes, Nomar Mazara, Gleyber Torres

You can hear the drool puddling on the floor of the fantasy team's conference room from here. The Rockies popped Lavigne 42nd overall a few weeks after he graduated high school last summer, and it was a notable selection given his cold-weather roots and first base-only defensive profile. The earliest returns rewarded their resounding faith in his bat, however, as he pummeled Pioneer League pitching to a 98th percentile DRC+ among all Rookie ballers. A full-season debut should be on tap in 2019, with a subsequent promotion schedule that'll track pretty directly with his offensive progress from there.

| YEAR | TEAM | LVL | AGE | PA | DRC+ | VORP | BABIP | BRR | FRAA | WARP |
|---|---|---|---|---|---|---|---|---|---|---|
| 2018 | GJR | RK | 18 | 258 | 190 | 27.3 | .410 | -0.6 | 1B(53): -6.8 | 1.1 |
| 2019 | COL | MLB | 19 | 251 | 62 | -7.3 | .243 | -0.5 | 1B -2 | -1.0 |

## Brendan Rodgers  SS

Born: 08/09/96   Age: 22   Bats: R   Throws: R
Height: 6'0"   Weight: 180   Origin: Round 1, 2015 Draft (#3 overall)

| YEAR | TEAM | LVL | AGE | PA | R | 2B | 3B | HR | RBI | BB | K | SB | CS | AVG/OBP/SLG |
|---|---|---|---|---|---|---|---|---|---|---|---|---|---|---|
| 2016 | ASH | A | 19 | 491 | 73 | 31 | 0 | 19 | 73 | 35 | 98 | 6 | 3 | .281/.342/.480 |
| 2017 | HFD | AA | 20 | 164 | 20 | 5 | 0 | 6 | 17 | 8 | 36 | 0 | 2 | .260/.323/.413 |
| 2017 | LNC | A+ | 20 | 236 | 44 | 21 | 3 | 12 | 47 | 6 | 35 | 2 | 1 | .387/.407/.671 |
| 2018 | HFD | AA | 21 | 402 | 49 | 23 | 2 | 17 | 62 | 30 | 76 | 12 | 3 | .275/.342/.493 |
| 2018 | ABQ | AAA | 21 | 72 | 5 | 4 | 0 | 0 | 5 | 1 | 16 | 0 | 0 | .232/.264/.290 |
| 2019 | COL | MLB | 22 | 35 | 3 | 2 | 0 | 1 | 4 | 1 | 9 | 0 | 0 | .212/.235/.364 |

Breakout: 19%   Improve: 44%   Collapse: 2%   Attrition: 24%   MLB: 52%
Comparables: Nick Franklin, Alen Hanson, Reid Brignac

It's always exciting when a long-touted prospect hops up the porch steps and sidles up to the door. All the more when the player's faults are evident but he might be so good that they don't matter. Rodgers' elite barrel skills have long been evident, especially given how frequently he has shown them off. The aggressiveness has been understandable: When an abundance of natural hitting talent and confidence gets dropped into bandbox after bandbox, sometimes very small walk rates and some bad habits happen. And sometimes a 150-ish DRC+ happens. Challenged by advanced assignments at every turn, Rodgers has thrived and marched on. Consensus remains that of a perfectly fine, okay, it'll do shortstop, though he probably works best with reps all over the dirt and the Rockies have increasingly nodded in that direction with his deployments. With their left side set for one more year the Rockies will have the luxury to oblige some additional high-minors seasoning, though an early forced entrance should not surprise.

| YEAR | TEAM | LVL | AGE | PA | DRC+ | VORP | BABIP | BRR | FRAA | WARP |
|---|---|---|---|---|---|---|---|---|---|---|
| 2016 | ASH | A | 19 | 491 | 113 | 21.9 | .319 | -2.5 | SS(56): 0.0, 2B(24): 0.9 | 1.0 |
| 2017 | HFD | AA | 20 | 164 | 100 | 6.5 | .306 | -0.5 | SS(33): -1.2, 2B(6): 0.3 | 0.2 |
| 2017 | LNC | A+ | 20 | 236 | 174 | 26.5 | .413 | 0.9 | SS(47): -5.6, 2B(4): -0.6 | 1.6 |
| 2018 | HFD | AA | 21 | 402 | 113 | 27.4 | .301 | 0.6 | SS(58): -6.7, 2B(21): -2.1 | 0.9 |
| 2018 | ABQ | AAA | 21 | 72 | 49 | -2.8 | .302 | -0.3 | SS(11): -1.8, 3B(4): -0.2 | -0.5 |
| 2019 | COL | MLB | 22 | 35 | 28 | -1.8 | .261 | 0.0 | 2B 0 | -0.2 |

## Raimel Tapia  OF

Born: 02/04/94  Age: 25  Bats: L  Throws: L
Height: 6'2"  Weight: 180  Origin: International Free Agent, 2010

| YEAR | TEAM | LVL | AGE | PA | R | 2B | 3B | HR | RBI | BB | K | SB | CS | AVG/OBP/SLG |
|---|---|---|---|---|---|---|---|---|---|---|---|---|---|---|
| 2016 | NBR | AAX | 22 | 457 | 79 | 20 | 5 | 8 | 34 | 25 | 49 | 17 | 14 | .323/.363/.450 |
| 2016 | ABQ | AAA | 22 | 110 | 14 | 5 | 5 | 0 | 14 | 2 | 12 | 6 | 3 | .346/.355/.490 |
| 2016 | COL | MLB | 22 | 41 | 4 | 0 | 0 | 0 | 3 | 2 | 11 | 3 | 0 | .263/.293/.263 |
| 2017 | ABQ | AAA | 23 | 277 | 45 | 20 | 8 | 2 | 30 | 13 | 42 | 12 | 2 | .369/.397/.529 |
| 2017 | COL | MLB | 23 | 171 | 27 | 12 | 2 | 2 | 16 | 8 | 36 | 5 | 2 | .288/.329/.425 |
| 2018 | ABQ | AAA | 24 | 473 | 81 | 33 | 9 | 11 | 62 | 32 | 85 | 21 | 3 | .302/.352/.495 |
| 2018 | COL | MLB | 24 | 27 | 6 | 2 | 1 | 1 | 6 | 2 | 7 | 0 | 0 | .200/.259/.480 |
| 2019 | COL | MLB | 25 | 374 | 48 | 19 | 5 | 9 | 38 | 18 | 76 | 12 | 4 | .272/.311/.433 |

Breakout: 10%   Improve: 57%   Collapse: 2%   Attrition: 40%   MLB: 72%
Comparables: Kevin Pillar, Andrew Toles, A.J. Pollock

Some players just kind of always are who you thought they were, and it's a path down which Tapia certainly appears poised to tread. While the stringbean frame isn't *quite* as stringy as it was once upon a time, the basic physicality appears set in stone. He's going to hit, potentially very well. He's going to hold his speed, and likely continue to refine it as he has throughout his development. It might be a bit of a tweener profile, but his glove should be more or less fine in whichever chunk of outfield grass it gets assigned. He's also out of options, and really it's just as well because the Pacific Coast League doesn't appear to have much else to teach him. Whether he'll learn more about big-league life in Colorado's everyday lineup remains to be seen, but one way or another it's nigh on time to see what the kid can do.

| YEAR | TEAM | LVL | AGE | PA | DRC+ | VORP | BABIP | BRR | FRAA | WARP |
|---|---|---|---|---|---|---|---|---|---|---|
| 2016 | NBR | AAX | 22 | 457 | 130 | 25.2 | .349 | 1.4 | | 2.1 |
| 2016 | ABQ | AAA | 22 | 110 | 85 | 2.9 | .379 | 0.0 | CF(12): 1.9, LF(8): 1.3 | 0.3 |
| 2016 | COL | MLB | 22 | 41 | 71 | -0.4 | .357 | 1.2 | CF(9): 0.2, LF(2): -0.2 | 0.1 |
| 2017 | ABQ | AAA | 23 | 277 | 123 | 18.9 | .432 | -0.1 | CF(48): 0.0, LF(5): -0.6 | 1.2 |
| 2017 | COL | MLB | 23 | 171 | 80 | 4.0 | .361 | 1.6 | RF(22): -3.0, LF(18): -1.3 | -0.3 |
| 2018 | ABQ | AAA | 24 | 473 | 99 | 16.1 | .354 | 1.4 | CF(65): -5.2, RF(24): 0.0 | 0.2 |
| 2018 | COL | MLB | 24 | 27 | 87 | 0.7 | .235 | 0.7 | CF(6): -0.4, RF(1): 0.0 | 0.1 |
| 2019 | COL | MLB | 25 | 374 | 92 | 10.6 | .320 | 1.4 | LF -2, RF 1 | 0.8 |

## Ryan Vilade  SS

Born: 02/18/99   Age: 20   Bats: R   Throws: R
Height: 6'2"   Weight: 194   Origin: Round 2, 2017 Draft (#48 overall)

| YEAR | TEAM | LVL | AGE | PA | R | 2B | 3B | HR | RBI | BB | K | SB | CS | AVG/OBP/SLG |
|---|---|---|---|---|---|---|---|---|---|---|---|---|---|---|
| 2017 | GJR | RK | 18 | 146 | 23 | 3 | 2 | 5 | 21 | 27 | 31 | 5 | 5 | .308/.438/.496 |
| 2018 | ASH | A | 19 | 533 | 77 | 20 | 4 | 5 | 44 | 49 | 96 | 17 | 13 | .274/.353/.368 |
| 2019 | COL | MLB | 20 | 251 | 25 | 3 | 0 | 6 | 20 | 16 | 72 | 3 | 2 | .176/.225/.267 |

Breakout: 9%   Improve: 9%   Collapse: 0%   Attrition: 1%   MLB: 9%
Comparables: Ruben Tejada, Tyler Wade, Orlando Arcia

If this were a regular ol' column on the internet, this is the part where we would pause to insert a bunch of those flashing siren light emojis in order to broadcast to the world that Vilade is the proverbial SON OF A COACH. Blessed with all of the feels for the game, baseball instinct and #want that such progeny often exude, the former second-rounder rebounded after a tough start to the season at Low-A. There's a lot to like in his advanced hitting approach, and while precious little of his power has wandered into professional games as yet, it's in there, and there's likely to be more of it coming as he finishes filling out a platonic ideal of a baseball frame. It's likely he'll have to move off the six spot when that happens, but if the bat turns into what the Rockies think it will, that detail won't much matter.

| YEAR | TEAM | LVL | AGE | PA | DRC+ | VORP | BABIP | BRR | FRAA | WARP |
|---|---|---|---|---|---|---|---|---|---|---|
| 2017 | GJR | RK | 18 | 146 | 130 | 13.9 | .378 | 0.4 | SS(30): -2.1 | 0.6 |
| 2018 | ASH | A | 19 | 533 | 113 | 25.8 | .333 | -1.9 | SS(116): -6.3 | 1.1 |
| 2019 | COL | MLB | 20 | 251 | 32 | -11.2 | .219 | -0.3 | SS -2 | -1.4 |

### Colton Welker 3B
Born: 10/09/97  Age: 21  Bats: R  Throws: R
Height: 6'2"  Weight: 195  Origin: Round 4, 2016 Draft (#110 overall)

| YEAR | TEAM | LVL | AGE | PA | R | 2B | 3B | HR | RBI | BB | K | SB | CS | AVG/OBP/SLG |
|---|---|---|---|---|---|---|---|---|---|---|---|---|---|---|
| 2016 | GJR | RK | 18 | 227 | 38 | 15 | 2 | 5 | 36 | 13 | 28 | 6 | 4 | .329/.366/.490 |
| 2017 | ASH | A | 19 | 279 | 32 | 18 | 1 | 6 | 33 | 18 | 42 | 5 | 7 | .350/.401/.500 |
| 2018 | LNC | A+ | 20 | 509 | 74 | 32 | 0 | 13 | 82 | 42 | 103 | 5 | 1 | .333/.383/.489 |
| 2019 | COL | MLB | 21 | 251 | 22 | 10 | 0 | 7 | 28 | 7 | 60 | 0 | 0 | .234/.256/.359 |

Breakout: 7%  Improve: 13%  Collapse: 0%  Attrition: 12%  MLB: 14%
Comparables: Cheslor Cuthbert, Jeimer Candelario, Wilmer Flores

To see the sheer violence in Welker's swing, especially when he's launching balls off the lunar reservation in Lancaster during batting practice, you'd be forgiven for having set the over/under on his High-A dingers at something approaching the Antelope Valley's 2,500-foot elevation. That didn't happen, though, despite a full season at the level. It hasn't happened anywhere for Welker, actually; the former fourth-rounder's raw power has thus far barked worse than it has bitten in games. And that's okay! He's hit at least .329 in each of his three professional seasons, displaying underlying hand-eye coordination and bat-to-ball skills that tickle the scouting senses. The hot corner defense has been a bit better than anticipated, too. It's an exciting package of talent moving through the minors on a just-as-exciting timeline.

| YEAR | TEAM | LVL | AGE | PA | DRC+ | VORP | BABIP | BRR | FRAA | WARP |
|---|---|---|---|---|---|---|---|---|---|---|
| 2016 | GJR | RK | 18 | 227 | 138 | 20.3 | .356 | -0.4 | 3B(48): -5.8 | 0.3 |
| 2017 | ASH | A | 19 | 279 | 153 | 19.6 | .399 | -1.6 | 3B(52): -7.3 | 1.0 |
| 2018 | LNC | A+ | 20 | 509 | 139 | 30.0 | .395 | 1.1 | 3B(92): -9.3, 1B(6): -0.7 | 1.2 |
| 2019 | COL | MLB | 21 | 251 | 65 | -5.5 | .281 | -0.6 | 3B -6, 1B 0 | -1.3 |

## Ben Bowden  LHP

Born: 10/21/94  Age: 24  Bats: L  Throws: L
Height: 6'4"  Weight: 235  Origin: Round 2, 2016 Draft (#45 overall)

| YEAR | TEAM | LVL | AGE | W | L | SV | G | GS | IP | H | HR | BB/9 | K/9 | K | GB% | BABIP |
|---|---|---|---|---|---|---|---|---|---|---|---|---|---|---|---|---|
| 2016 | ASH | A | 21 | 0 | 1 | 0 | 26 | 0 | 23² | 23 | 1 | 5.7 | 11.0 | 29 | 43% | .373 |
| 2018 | ASH | A | 23 | 3 | 0 | 0 | 15 | 0 | 15¹ | 17 | 2 | 2.9 | 14.7 | 25 | 43% | .429 |
| 2018 | LNC | A+ | 23 | 4 | 2 | 0 | 34 | 0 | 36² | 35 | 6 | 3.7 | 13.0 | 53 | 35% | .337 |
| 2019 | COL | MLB | 24 | 2 | 1 | 1 | 35 | 0 | 36² | 36 | 5 | 5.3 | 10.1 | 41 | 37% | .332 |

Breakout: 0%   Improve: 0%   Collapse: 2%   Attrition: 2%   MLB: 2%
Comparables: Brian Schlitter, Neil Wagner, Josh Fields

During the Great New England Shoemakers' Strike of 1860 in Bowden's home town of Lynn, Massachusetts, women protesting labor injustice marched through a blizzard with signs that read "Give Us a Fair Compensation and We Will Labor Cheerfully." Bowden got a head start on the former, inking an above-slot deal high in the second round back in 2016. Injuries prevented his labor, cheerful or otherwise, in 2017, but he got back on the bump for 52 solid innings out of a couple A-ball bullpens last year. It's a strong three-pitch mix from the left side, but the north-south nature of his sequencing and wandering in-zone command led to more squared offerings than ideal. The stuff was back, however, in all its bat-missing glory. And there's fast-track bullpen potential here if it's back for good.

| YEAR | TEAM | LVL | AGE | WHIP | ERA | DRA | WARP | MPH | FB% | WHF | CSP |
|---|---|---|---|---|---|---|---|---|---|---|---|
| 2016 | ASH | A | 21 | 1.61 | 3.04 | 3.99 | 0.2 | | | | |
| 2018 | ASH | A | 23 | 1.43 | 3.52 | 3.21 | 0.3 | | | | |
| 2018 | LNC | A+ | 23 | 1.36 | 4.17 | 4.64 | 0.1 | | | | |
| 2019 | COL | MLB | 24 | 1.56 | 4.70 | 5.16 | -0.1 | | | | |

## Ryan Castellani  RHP

Born: 04/01/96   Age: 23   Bats: R   Throws: R
Height: 6'4"   Weight: 220   Origin: Round 2, 2014 Draft (#48 overall)

| YEAR | TEAM | LVL | AGE | W | L | SV | G | GS | IP | H | HR | BB/9 | K/9 | K | GB% | BABIP |
|---|---|---|---|---|---|---|---|---|---|---|---|---|---|---|---|---|
| 2016 | MOD | A+ | 20 | 7 | 8 | 0 | 26 | 26 | $167^2$ | 156 | 8 | 2.7 | 7.6 | 142 | 55% | .302 |
| 2017 | HFD | AA | 21 | 9 | 12 | 0 | 27 | 27 | $157^1$ | 163 | 16 | 2.7 | 7.6 | 132 | 47% | .309 |
| 2018 | HFD | AA | 22 | 7 | 9 | 0 | 26 | 26 | $134^1$ | 135 | 15 | 4.7 | 6.1 | 91 | 39% | .291 |
| 2019 | COL | MLB | 23 | 1 | 1 | 0 | 3 | 3 | 14 | 15 | 2 | 3.9 | 7.5 | 12 | 42% | .296 |

Breakout: 14%   Improve: 22%   Collapse: 8%   Attrition: 25%   MLB: 34%
Comparables: Duane Underwood, Jayson Aquino, Drew VerHagen

Colorado pushed their 2014 second-rounder aggressively up the low-minors ladder for a couple years after drafting him out of high school, but that trajectory ground to a screeching halt when Castellani struggled with his Double-A assignment in 2017. Given a second chance to try the level again in 2018, he struggled again. A full wind and stabbing, deep arm action are pages out of Max Scherzer's playbook, and it's a reminder that you have to be *Max Scherzer* to make those mechanics work. But he'll still show flashes of a three-pitch mix that looks real good in sporadic bursts of proper execution and location. An addition to the club's 40-man roster over the winter, he'll play at 23 with at least one more year to find it and force his way up the organizational depth chart.

| YEAR | TEAM | LVL | AGE | WHIP | ERA | DRA | WARP | MPH | FB% | WHF | CSP |
|---|---|---|---|---|---|---|---|---|---|---|---|
| 2016 | MOD | A+ | 20 | 1.23 | 3.81 | 3.63 | 3.5 | | | | |
| 2017 | HFD | AA | 21 | 1.33 | 4.81 | 4.19 | 1.8 | | | | |
| 2018 | HFD | AA | 22 | 1.53 | 5.49 | 5.32 | 0.0 | | | | |
| 2019 | COL | MLB | 23 | 1.51 | 5.03 | 5.23 | 0.0 | | | | |

## D.J. Johnson  RHP

Born: 08/30/89   Age: 29   Bats: L   Throws: R
Height: 6'4"   Weight: 235   Origin: Undrafted Free Agent, 2010

| YEAR | TEAM | LVL | AGE | W | L | SV | G | GS | IP | H | HR | BB/9 | K/9 | K | GB% | BABIP |
|---|---|---|---|---|---|---|---|---|---|---|---|---|---|---|---|---|
| 2016 | ARK | AA | 26 | 4 | 4 | 6 | 47 | 1 | 69$^1$ | 78 | 1 | 4.2 | 8.7 | 67 | 51% | .374 |
| 2017 | HFD | AA | 27 | 1 | 1 | 4 | 43 | 0 | 64$^1$ | 53 | 4 | 3.4 | 7.1 | 51 | 59% | .265 |
| 2018 | ABQ | AAA | 28 | 3 | 5 | 18 | 50 | 0 | 55$^1$ | 56 | 5 | 2.4 | 13.7 | 84 | 44% | .398 |
| 2018 | COL | MLB | 28 | 1 | 0 | 0 | 7 | 0 | 6$^1$ | 6 | 0 | 2.8 | 12.8 | 9 | 38% | .375 |
| 2019 | COL | MLB | 29 | 1 | 1 | 0 | 25 | 0 | 26 | 27 | 3 | 3.9 | 9.5 | 28 | 46% | .312 |

Breakout: 8%   Improve: 10%   Collapse: 7%   Attrition: 14%   MLB: 19%
Comparables: Jess Todd, Layne Somsen, Jose Valdez

Just your run-of-the-mill undrafted free agent who came out of minor-league bullpens for five different organizations across more than 270 affiliated appearances, beach bummed two tours of indy ball, tore his pitching shoulder apart, worked in a Scioto County lumber mill when it looked like he might not get another shot, got another shot, threw one season, then a full 32-game winter season in Mexico, then kept throwing right on into another season, and finally Beatrix Kiddo'ed his way onto a big-league mound a mile high in the sky. Johnson struck out both hitters he faced in his major league debut. Then he made the postseason roster instead of the club's Opening Day starter. He struck out a couple more hitters when he pitched in October, too. Unreal. He sits 94 with a wipeout slider and all the time in the world.

| YEAR | TEAM | LVL | AGE | WHIP | ERA | DRA | WARP | MPH | FB% | WHF | CSP |
|---|---|---|---|---|---|---|---|---|---|---|---|
| 2016 | ARK | AA | 26 | 1.59 | 4.02 | 4.14 | 0.5 | | | | |
| 2017 | HFD | AA | 27 | 1.20 | 2.80 | 3.87 | 0.7 | | | | |
| 2018 | ABQ | AAA | 28 | 1.28 | 3.90 | 2.74 | 1.5 | | | | |
| 2018 | COL | MLB | 28 | 1.26 | 4.26 | 4.70 | 0.0 | 95.3 | 44.8 | 16.2 | 44.8 |
| 2019 | COL | MLB | 29 | 1.47 | 4.16 | 4.31 | 0.2 | 94.6 | 44.8 | 16.2 | 44.8 |

## Colorado Rockies 2019

**Peter Lambert   RHP**
Born: 04/18/97   Age: 22   Bats: R   Throws: R
Height: 6'2"   Weight: 185   Origin: Round 2, 2015 Draft (#44 overall)

| YEAR | TEAM | LVL | AGE | W | L | SV | G | GS | IP | H | HR | BB/9 | K/9 | K | GB% | BABIP |
|---|---|---|---|---|---|---|---|---|---|---|---|---|---|---|---|---|
| 2016 | ASH | A | 19 | 5 | 8 | 0 | 26 | 26 | 126 | 125 | 7 | 2.4 | 7.7 | 108 | 47% | .324 |
| 2017 | LNC | A+ | 20 | 9 | 8 | 0 | 26 | 26 | 142$^1$ | 147 | 18 | 1.9 | 8.3 | 131 | 43% | .321 |
| 2018 | HFD | AA | 21 | 8 | 2 | 0 | 15 | 15 | 92$^2$ | 80 | 6 | 1.2 | 7.3 | 75 | 50% | .282 |
| 2018 | ABQ | AAA | 21 | 2 | 5 | 0 | 11 | 11 | 55$^1$ | 72 | 5 | 2.4 | 5.0 | 31 | 52% | .345 |
| 2019 | COL | MLB | 22 | 1 | 1 | 0 | 3 | 3 | 15 | 16 | 2 | 2.6 | 6.8 | 11 | 43% | .296 |

Breakout: 15%   Improve: 23%   Collapse: 8%   Attrition: 22%   MLB: 41%
Comparables: Ariel Jurado, Enyel De Los Santos, Will Smith

With a spate of recent graduations and standard attrition around him, Lambert's claim as the organization's best pitching prospect isn't an especially controversial one. Whether the pedigree can translate to palatable big-league innings in the harshest of environments remains to be seen, though he's tamed such elements before. Eleven strikeout-challenged starts at Triple-A reminded us of his limitations, specifically the lack of a true bat-misser among his four pitches. But he made those starts at the same age as most college juniors, and his strike-throwing and tenacity are the stuff of a legitimate big-league starter. He should garner his first opportunity to fulfill that destiny in 2019.

| YEAR | TEAM | LVL | AGE | WHIP | ERA | DRA | WARP | MPH | FB% | WHF | CSP |
|---|---|---|---|---|---|---|---|---|---|---|---|
| 2016 | ASH | A | 19 | 1.25 | 3.93 | 6.30 | -2.0 | | | | |
| 2017 | LNC | A+ | 20 | 1.24 | 4.17 | 3.92 | 2.2 | | | | |
| 2018 | HFD | AA | 21 | 0.99 | 2.23 | 4.53 | 0.9 | | | | |
| 2018 | ABQ | AAA | 21 | 1.57 | 5.04 | 4.62 | 0.6 | | | | |
| 2019 | COL | MLB | 22 | 1.39 | 4.65 | 4.84 | 0.0 | | | | |

**Riley Pint  RHP**
Born: 11/06/97   Age: 21   Bats: R   Throws: R
Height: 6'4"   Weight: 195   Origin: Round 1, 2016 Draft (#4 overall)

| YEAR | TEAM | LVL | AGE | W | L | SV | G | GS | IP | H | HR | BB/9 | K/9 | K | GB% | BABIP |
|---|---|---|---|---|---|---|---|---|---|---|---|---|---|---|---|---|
| 2016 | GJR | RK | 18 | 1 | 5 | 0 | 11 | 11 | 37 | 43 | 2 | 5.6 | 8.8 | 36 | 60% | .383 |
| 2017 | ASH | A | 19 | 2 | 11 | 0 | 22 | 22 | 93 | 96 | 3 | 5.7 | 7.6 | 79 | 60% | .325 |
| 2018 | BOI | A- | 20 | 0 | 2 | 0 | 3 | 3 | 8 | 4 | 0 | 10.1 | 9.0 | 8 | 47% | .235 |
| 2019 | COL | MLB | 21 | 2 | 3 | 0 | 8 | 8 | 31$^1$ | 34 | 4 | 7.8 | 7.3 | 25 | 46% | .330 |

Breakout: 1%   Improve: 1%   Collapse: 0%   Attrition: 2%   MLB: 2%
Comparables: Elvin Ramirez, Greg Reynolds, James Houser

Look, it was *always* going to be a process, from the moment Colorado popped Pint fourth overall a couple years back. He's a big dude, still growing into his big dude body, and his stuff moves just a disgusting amount. That's a recipe for lagging command and a slow growth curve if ever you've seen one. And sure enough, here we are where we are today. Pint made precious little progress refining his craft last year, staggering instead through a forearm scare and an oblique strain that combined to drink up just about the full season. The peaks of the Rocky Mountains themselves still look up at Pint's ceiling; pitchers with elite fastballs and the potential for three average-or-better secondaries don't grow on trees, after all. He'll hope for a healthy camp and healthier mechanics in 2019, while a thirsty pack of TINSTAAPP truthers gather and circle.

| YEAR | TEAM | LVL | AGE | WHIP | ERA | DRA | WARP | MPH | FB% | WHF | CSP |
|---|---|---|---|---|---|---|---|---|---|---|---|
| 2016 | GJR | RK | 18 | 1.78 | 5.35 | 4.48 | 0.5 | | | | |
| 2017 | ASH | A | 19 | 1.67 | 5.42 | 4.58 | 0.8 | | | | |
| 2018 | BOI | A- | 20 | 1.62 | 1.12 | 4.88 | 0.0 | | | | |
| 2019 | COL | MLB | 21 | 1.98 | 6.11 | 6.74 | -0.5 | | | | |

## Ryan Rolison  LHP

Born: 07/11/97  Age: 21  Bats: R  Throws: L
Height: 6'2"  Weight: 195  Origin: Round 1, 2018 Draft (#22 overall)

| YEAR | TEAM | LVL | AGE | W | L | SV | G | GS | IP | H | HR | BB/9 | K/9 | K | GB% | BABIP |
|---|---|---|---|---|---|---|---|---|---|---|---|---|---|---|---|---|
| 2018 | GJR | RK | 20 | 0 | 1 | 0 | 9 | 9 | 29 | 15 | 2 | 2.5 | 10.6 | 34 | 66% | .200 |
| 2019 | COL | MLB | 21 | 2 | 2 | 0 | 9 | 9 | 33² | 36 | 4 | 4.9 | 8.0 | 30 | 56% | .331 |

Comparables: Thyago Vieira, Yency Almonte, Kendry Flores

The Rockies called Rolison's number with the 22nd overall pick last June, and when they did they brought on board one of the more polished arms in the draft class. The performance in a two-year career at Mississippi was more solid than spectacular, but the raw ingredients are much better than that, including one of the better curveballs in the collegiate ranks and a well-proportioned, athletic frame that should eventually allow repeatable mechanics to take hold. Each of the left-hander's four pitches already suggests average-or-better value down the line, and the combination proved much too difficult for Pioneer League hitters to handle during a brief slate of action after signing. He should see plenty of full-season ball in his first full year among professionals.

| YEAR | TEAM | LVL | AGE | WHIP | ERA | DRA | WARP | MPH | FB% | WHF | CSP |
|---|---|---|---|---|---|---|---|---|---|---|---|
| 2018 | GJR | RK | 20 | 0.79 | 1.86 | 3.40 | 0.8 | | | | |
| 2019 | COL | MLB | 21 | 1.60 | 4.61 | 5.07 | 0.1 | | | | |

# LINEOUTS

## Hitters

| HITTER | POS | TEAM | LVL | AGE | PA | R | 2B | 3B | HR | RBI | BB | K | SB | CS | AVG/OBP/SLG | DRC+ | WARP |
|---|---|---|---|---|---|---|---|---|---|---|---|---|---|---|---|---|---|
| Willie Abreu | RF | BOI | A- | 23 | 41 | 3 | 2 | 0 | 0 | 3 | 3 | 9 | 2 | 0 | .162/.225/.216 | 60 | -0.1 |
| | RF | LNC | A+ | 23 | 277 | 41 | 12 | 2 | 7 | 27 | 20 | 62 | 19 | 9 | .266/.322/.413 | 90 | -1.0 |
| Noel Cuevas | RF | ABQ | AAA | 26 | 177 | 17 | 10 | 4 | 5 | 29 | 16 | 23 | 3 | 5 | .331/.390/.538 | 126 | 0.1 |
| | RF | COL | MLB | 26 | 153 | 16 | 4 | 1 | 2 | 10 | 6 | 24 | 1 | 0 | .233/.268/.315 | 76 | -0.3 |
| Yonathan Daza | CF | HFD | AA | 24 | 228 | 27 | 18 | 2 | 4 | 29 | 7 | 24 | 4 | 5 | .306/.330/.461 | 118 | 1.1 |
| Eddy Diaz | SS | DCR | Rk | 18 | 223 | 57 | 13 | 5 | 0 | 24 | 31 | 17 | 54 | 8 | .309/.417/.436 | 154 | 2.4 |
| Vince Fernandez | LF | LNC | A+ | 22 | 499 | 82 | 25 | 8 | 24 | 75 | 65 | 172 | 10 | 5 | .265/.370/.532 | 112 | 2.2 |
| Josh Fuentes | 3B | ABQ | AAA | 25 | 586 | 93 | 39 | 12 | 14 | 95 | 21 | 103 | 3 | 5 | .327/.354/.517 | 110 | 2.7 |
| Daniel Montano | CF | DCR | Rk | 19 | 51 | 4 | 2 | 0 | 1 | 8 | 5 | 5 | 2 | 0 | .182/.275/.295 | 93 | 0.0 |
| | CF | GJR | Rk | 19 | 264 | 32 | 15 | 5 | 4 | 29 | 21 | 57 | 9 | 5 | .279/.338/.433 | 83 | -1.4 |
| Brian Mundell | 1B | HFD | AA | 24 | 506 | 49 | 25 | 1 | 7 | 41 | 53 | 77 | 1 | 3 | .263/.345/.372 | 102 | 0.8 |
| Tyler Nevin | 1B | LNC | A+ | 21 | 417 | 59 | 25 | 1 | 13 | 62 | 34 | 77 | 4 | 3 | .328/.386/.503 | 140 | 0.8 |
| Dom Nunez | C | HFD | AA | 23 | 377 | 34 | 12 | 0 | 9 | 42 | 46 | 73 | 8 | 6 | .222/.320/.343 | 92 | 1.1 |
| Roberto Ramos | 1B | LNC | A+ | 23 | 255 | 44 | 15 | 3 | 17 | 43 | 32 | 65 | 3 | 1 | .304/.411/.640 | 160 | 1.2 |
| | 1B | HFD | AA | 23 | 228 | 26 | 9 | 0 | 15 | 34 | 26 | 75 | 2 | 1 | .231/.320/.503 | 117 | 0.2 |
| Wes Rogers | OF | HFD | AA | 24 | 197 | 17 | 4 | 1 | 2 | 15 | 15 | 44 | 14 | 4 | .200/.269/.269 | 49 | -0.7 |
| | OF | LNC | A+ | 24 | 206 | 30 | 8 | 0 | 6 | 34 | 17 | 48 | 10 | 3 | .286/.345/.427 | 102 | -0.3 |
| Terrin Vavra | SS | BOI | A- | 21 | 199 | 22 | 8 | 4 | 4 | 26 | 26 | 40 | 9 | 1 | .302/.396/.467 | 143 | 0.7 |

**Willie Abreu** looks and sometimes moves like a linebacker, but also doesn't quite hit with the oomph you'd expect from someone with his size and swing path. This concludes this test of the Future Fourth Outfielder Alert System. ⓥ The organization's highest-paid J2 signee last summer, **Warming Bernabel** has the chance to be a global superstar, though climate scientists might be warning about the waters rising to Denver by the time the 16-year-old reaches the majors. ⓥ A 21st-round selection presaged a journey of nearly eight years and almost 800 minor-league games before **Noel Cuevas** finally staggered onto a big-league field. But after his right-handed bat provided negative value against left-handed pitching (in Coors, no less), it might take that long for him to garner another shot. ⓥ Injuries dampened the follow-up to a breakout 2017 campaign, but **Yonathan Daza** continued to impress defensively at Double-A while flashing enough bat-to-ball to suggest a future 25-man role. ⓥ Colorado paid $750,000 to procure **Eddy Diaz**'s talents on the international market, and while DSL stats are overwhelmingly useless, his 84 stolen bases in 87 professional games at an 86-percent clip is some kinda alliterative something. He'll be stateside this year. ⓥ **Vince Fernandez** produced the most Lancaster season of any hitter last year, but a whole bunch of empty swings at fat pitches in the zone suggest we should temper expectations for him in Double-A. ⓥ Nolan Arenado's cousin went undrafted out of college, but here we are half a decade later and **Josh**

**Fuentes** hasn't really ever stopped hitting, including all year at Albuquerque and throughout the Arizona Fall League. There's a decent chance he tags in for Nolan in his big-league debut, and that's just a plain old cool baseball thing. ⚾ A $2 million bonus baby once upon a time, **Daniel Montano** held his own in his stateside debut and might eventually, some day, grow old enough to hoist a pint to celebrate the performance. ⚾ The 24-year-old right-handed first base-only guys who slug .372 in Double-A do not, typically, top prospects make. And 25-year-olds who reprise that line tend more often than not to find themselves touring organizational depth charts from Hartford to Hanwha. So this year's a big one for **Brian Mundell**. ⚾ Patient and powerful like his dad, **Tyler Nevin** has battled significant injuries throughout his career, including two DL stints last season. He crushed California and Arizona Fall League pitching alike after returning from the most recent one though, and his bat might just be enough to carve out a big-league path if he can stay on the field. ⚾ On one hand, the bar for backup catcher offense has been set extremely low in Colorado (thanks, Tony Wolters). On the other, **Dom Nunez** might just test those limits if ever granted the opportunity. ⚾ **Roberto Ramos** won the Cal League home run derby and three-true-outcomed his way to Double-A, where he'll find long-term comfort unless the bat really maxes out. ⚾ It's Terrance Gore's world, and **Wes Rogers** is just hoping to one day live in it. ⚾ Back issues crunched his collegiate career, but third-rounder **Terrin Vavra** impressed with a broad base of skills in his pro debut.

## Pitchers

| PITCHER | TEAM | LVL | AGE | W | L | SV | G | GS | IP | H | HR | BB/9 | K/9 | K | GB% | WHIP | ERA | DRA | WARP |
|---|---|---|---|---|---|---|---|---|---|---|---|---|---|---|---|---|---|---|---|
| Carlos Estevez | ABQ | AAA | 25 | 0 | 1 | 1 | 28 | 0 | $28^1$ | 37 | 6 | 3.5 | 11.1 | 35 | 39% | 1.69 | 6.35 | 3.44 | 0.5 |
| Rico Garcia | LNC | A+ | 24 | 7 | 7 | 0 | 16 | 15 | 100 | 99 | 12 | 2.0 | 9.1 | 101 | 46% | 1.21 | 3.42 | 4.28 | 1.2 |
|  | HFD | AA | 24 | 6 | 2 | 0 | 11 | 11 | 67 | 54 | 8 | 2.7 | 8.2 | 61 | 44% | 1.10 | 2.28 | 4.18 | 0.9 |
| Rayan Gonzalez | HFD | AA | 27 | 0 | 1 | 0 | 19 | 0 | $17^1$ | 19 | 4 | 4.2 | 8.8 | 17 | 44% | 1.56 | 5.19 | 5.09 | 0.0 |
| Sam Howard | ABQ | AAA | 25 | 3 | 8 | 0 | 21 | 21 | 96 | 106 | 13 | 3.2 | 7.5 | 80 | 40% | 1.46 | 5.06 | 4.85 | 0.8 |
|  | COL | MLB | 25 | 0 | 0 | 0 | 4 | 0 | 4 | 5 | 0 | 6.8 | 2.2 | 1 | 53% | 2.00 | 2.25 | 8.49 | -0.2 |
| Reid Humphreys | LNC | A+ | 23 | 2 | 0 | 22 | 35 | 0 | $34^1$ | 22 | 1 | 3.4 | 13.4 | 51 | 51% | 1.02 | 1.83 | 3.18 | 0.7 |
| Justin Lawrence | LNC | A+ | 23 | 0 | 2 | 11 | 55 | 0 | $54^1$ | 36 | 2 | 4.5 | 10.3 | 62 | 63% | 1.16 | 2.65 | 3.41 | 1.0 |
| Mike Nikorak | BOI | A- | 21 | 0 | 0 | 0 | 9 | 2 | $8^1$ | 7 | 0 | 11.9 | 10.8 | 10 | 55% | 2.16 | 4.32 | 4.16 | 0.1 |
| Jesus Tinoco | HFD | AA | 23 | 9 | 12 | 0 | 26 | 26 | 141 | 149 | 23 | 2.4 | 8.4 | 132 | 38% | 1.33 | 4.79 | 4.16 | 1.9 |
| Robert Tyler | ASH | A | 23 | 4 | 2 | 8 | 34 | 0 | $38^1$ | 37 | 5 | 1.6 | 12.2 | 52 | 62% | 1.15 | 3.99 | 2.85 | 0.9 |
|  | LNC | A+ | 23 | 0 | 1 | 0 | 12 | 0 | $9^1$ | 17 | 2 | 4.8 | 4.8 | 5 | 46% | 2.36 | 9.64 | 5.52 | -0.1 |

An anticipated piece of the bullpen puzzle entering the year, **Carlos Estevez** instead missed the first half of it with oblique and elbow issues, then got bit by the home run bug at Triple-A. The stuff remained intact on re-entry, and he'll try again to seize hold of a 25-man spot in 2019. ⚾ A former 30th-rounder, **Rico Garcia** up and tamed Lancaster for a hundred innings before holding his own in a half season of Double-A last year, and if that was his peak, he can lay claim to a better one than most. ⚾ The once-promising ascent of **Rayan Gonzalez** paused for the cause of a one-and-a-half-year Tommy John vacation, but he was back on the bump for a couple dozen rusty rehab runs in the season's second half. When healthy he'll pump mid-90s cheddar with cut and a boatload of groundballs on the back end. He could figure into the bullpen mix in Colorado this year. ⚾ Former third-rounder **Sam Howard**'s fringy fastball got knocked around again at Triple-A, and while he made his way to Denver for a couple cameos, the Rockies rewarded that debut with a post-season non-tender. ⚾ **Reid Humphreys**' nasty stuff—high-90s cheddar with a cutting cousin a few miles an hour slower—played its heart out at the launching pad in Lancaster, and if you can make it there, you can make it anywhere. ⚾ As if his funky delivery and the stilted visuals it produces for hitters weren't enough, **Justin Lawrence** sits high-90s with a wipeout slider. Nobody'll confuse him for Maddux, but it's effectively wild and a high-leverage profile in spite of it. ⚾ The Poconos sent its best to Colorado 27th overall in 2016, but **Mike Nikorak** famously left his control and a bunch of velocity back east after signing. A two-year vision quest in his elbow followed, spent mostly in recovery from Tommy John before finally getting back on a Pioneer League mound in August. ⚾ **Jesus Tinoco** has himself a heater and two hooks that can play nicely out of the 'pen. ⚾ A plus mid-90s fastball and solid, tumbling cambio highlight the arsenal for **Robert Tyler**, a former 38th-overall pick who spent the year in A-ball shaking off the rust of an injury-obliterated 2017.

# Rockies Prospects

**The State of the System:**
The prospect pipeline to Denver is slowing a bit, but there's still close-to-ready talent for the win-now Rockies. Well, we think they are trying to win now. The Rockies are always quite confusing.

**The Top Ten:**

**1** **Brendan Rodgers   SS**         OFP: 70   Likely: 55   ETA: Late 2019
Born: 08/09/96   Age: 22   Bats: R   Throws: R   Height: 6'0"   Weight: 180
Origin: Round 1, 2015 Draft (#3 overall)

**The Report:** After struggling during a brief Double-A cameo in 2017, Rodgers played more to the five-tool-shortstop scouting report in 2018. While he took full advantage of the friendly confines of Dunkin' Donuts park, Rodgers is a strong kid who generates plus raw power—although it's not easy per se, he has to work for it. And that means the swing can get a little stiff, making him vulnerable to velocity in his kitchen. Rodgers will go fishing against spin at times too, but he makes adjustments within at-bats and controls the barrel well enough to project an average hit tool. That should allow most of the plus raw power to play in games, even before we consider his future home park.

Rodgers is fine at shortstop, although you can tell he's battling the position at times. He has an above-average arm, but he's not as rangy as you'd like, and his actions can be a bit mechanical. The internal clock just seems slow at times in the field. He may have to slide to second if he loses any additional range, although he's an above-average runner at present. Rodgers is a guy I've sorta had to be talked into as a top tier prospect. I get it, but I've just never really seen it.

**The Risks:** Medium. Man, this feels like it should be 7/6, low. I just can't quite dispel the nagging voice in my head that thinks there's significant risk in the hit tool against major-league arms.

**Ben Carsley's Fantasy Take:** Once upon a time, Rodgers seemed a decent bet to some day be considered a top-3 dynasty prospect. While that may never come to pass, don't let prospect fatigue push you off of him completely. Rodgers is still an excellent fantasy asset who could routinely push for 25-plus homers from somewhere on the infield, and Coors may inflate his stats further. The real question for me is whether his hit tool will allow him to put up averages closer to .290 or .260, but either way Rodgers is a guy you want to own. We'll just have to wait and see if he ends up a solid cog or a true fantasy cornerstone.

### 2. Garrett Hampson  IF
OFP: 55   Likely: 50   ETA: Debuted in 2018
Born: 10/10/94   Age: 24   Bats: R   Throws: R   Height: 5'11"   Weight: 185
Origin: Round 3, 2016 Draft (#81 overall)

**The Report:** Hampson is a dirty uniform player, the kind who endears himself to scouts quickly. That type of dude generally doesn't move the "top prospect" needle, but calling him a "grinder"—which to be clear, definitely applies—does a bit of a disservice to just how good a baseball player he is. He's a borderline 7 runner and is hyper-aggressive on the basepaths while also picking his spots well. He'll nab 30 steals a year and won't get caught much. Hampson is not a natural shortstop, but he fights the position to a draw. He is rangy with good hands and instincts, and he's smooth around the bag. His arm is just a bit light for an everyday shortstop role, but he should have an above-average glove at second.

The hit tool is solid-average. Hampson is pesky at the plate, fouling stuff off and working counts. He'll take a walk, lean into a pitch running inside. He's a good bunter. The swing does have more moving parts than you'd like though. There's a big leg kick and a bit of a hitch, but he has above-average bat speed and just barrels everything. The one hole in the profile is power. Even in Coors, Hampson is gonna shoot balls gap-to-gap and try and take an extra base or two. He'll probably top out around 10 home runs or so most seasons. It's not a sexy profile and the only endorsement he'll be getting is from Tide, but Hampson will do a job for you, and he'll do it well. This is normally a prospect profile I look slightly askance at, but he endeared himself quickly to me too.

**The Risks:** Low. He has hit in the upper minors just like he hit in the lower minors and he has a strong case to be the Rockies Opening Day second baseman. I gave up trying to figure out how Colorado will handle young players years ago, though.

**Ben Carsley's Fantasy Take:** Bret and I (especially Bret) were aggressive in our rankings of Hampson last season, and whatdya know, blind squirrels, nuts, etc. Hampson is comfortably a top-25 dynasty prospect thanks to his proximity to the majors, speed-based upside, and insanely favorable contextual factors. Assuming he gets near-every day playing time, he could genuinely challenge for a top-10 finish at second base as soon as this season. There's definitely some danger that a slow start could see Hampson lose out on playing time, but that's something he'll eventually overcome; he's simply too good to be relegated to utility duty.

### 3. Ryan Rolison   LHP
OFP: 55   Likely: 50   ETA: 2021
Born: 07/11/97   Age: 21   Bats: R   Throws: L   Height: 6'2"   Weight: 195
Origin: Round 1, 2018 Draft (#22 overall)

**The Report:** Rolison ticks all the usual suspect boxes for a late first-round left-handed college arm. He hides the ball well and his low-90s fastball will sneak up on you. He can spot it to both sides and cut it occasionally, but the command is just average and his high arm slot produces only fringy wiggle. The party piece here is a potential plus curve that shows good tilt, but can get slurvy on occasion. Rolison's command of the curve outpaces his command of the fastball at times. He's got a sinking change as well, but he slows his arm speed and tends to spike it. The best ones flash average, and his feel for spin gives the pitch some projection despite being presently well below-average.

Rolison throws strikes and attacks hitters and is left-handed. The stuff is only average to solid-average, but he is polished and left-handed. He's not the most exciting member of the 2018 draft class, but he's one of the more likely ones to be a major-leaguer. Also, he's left-handed.

**The Risks:** Medium. He's a polished college lefty, albeit one with a very short pro track record.

**Ben Carsley's Fantasy Take:** From a dynasty perspective there is juuuuuust a little bit of a drop off from the top two names on this list to the third. In a neutral setting, Rolison would likely get lost in the glut of mid-rotation prospects we advise you not to invest heavily in every season. Add in that he's a Rockie and there's basically no need for you to pay him any mind. That may sound harsh, but it's got more to do with Rolison's circumstances than anything he's done himself. Kyle Freeland is the exception, not the rule.

### 4. Peter Lambert   RHP
OFP: 55   Likely: 50   ETA: Late 2019
Born: 04/18/97   Age: 22   Bats: R   Throws: R   Height: 6'2"   Weight: 185
Origin: Round 2, 2015 Draft (#44 overall)

**The Report:** Lambert is a command and pitchability righty. This is usually the type of prospect profile that forces me to stifle an involuntary yawn, but most command righties don't dominate Double-A the way the 21-year-old Lambert did. He's not a soft tosser, touching as high as 96 for me this year, but generally working 91-94. He'll cut it at times and there's enough movement and deception to keep it off the fat part of the barrel, but the pitch's efficacy is command over movement. Lambert throws the fastball to all four quadrants and is particularly effective changing eye levels.

The changeup is his best secondary, and it plays off the fastball well. It only features 5-6 mph of velocity separation, but the firmness makes it look like the fastball right up until it tumbles off the deck, and it flashes plus. Lambert also throws a slider and a curve. The curve is better at present, showing consistent 11-5 shape, but it's more of a spot than chase pitch at present, and can get a bit humpy at the lower end of it's 76-81 velo band. The slider is used occasionally for a different breaking ball look right-on-right, but functions more as a cutter. Lambert is a plus athlete, repeats well, throws strikes with everything, and fields his position well. There's a bit of projection left in his frame as well.

**The Risks:** Medium. Lambert is a righty command dude with an averagish fastball. He may not have a true major league out pitch, and uh, he's gonna pitch in a place that will punish that.

**Ben Carsley's Fantasy Take:** See Rolison, Ryan, but now imagine him as a righty.

### 5  Colton Welker   3B    OFP: 55   Likely: 50   ETA: 2020
Born: 10/09/97   Age: 21   Bats: R   Throws: R   Height: 6'2"   Weight: 195
Origin: Round 4, 2016 Draft (#110 overall)

**The Report:** Welker's hitting-count rips are a sight to behold, with a long, majestic bat path and the bat speed for the barrel to traverse it with impressive haste. It's all a bit of an illusion at present, however, as the approach into the zone is steeper and he leverages his attack angle less often than most young power hitters. High-end hand-eye and an intelligent, all-fields approach underlie an impressive hit tool that may push plus when all's said and done—minor-league statistical salt grains and all, but he's sitting on a .337 professional average in more than 900 at-bats now. Above-average game power will come with maturity, but for now he's a drill-it-on-a-line kinda guy, and that's a-ok.

Welker's thick frame and heavy legs aren't masking any hidden speed above his present 30 grade, but he's got the quickness and short-range agility to play a better third base than you'd expect. He gets down well on balls in reach, and a powerful crossover extends the range just enough. Above-average arm strength ties off a workable, solid-average defensive profile at the hot corner.

**The Risks:** Relatively low: This level-a-year prep bat has hit the ball consistently hard through each of his first three levels. The frame's on the bulkier side, but he showed strong work ethic all year and the physicality should work. The foundational hitting talent is strong enough that he's on a pretty straight path toward an everyday role at the highest level.

**Ben Carsley's Fantasy Take:** I actually like Welker a bit more than the write-up above suggests I should. I've long been a believer in his bat-to-ball ability, and even if the power hasn't shown up big time yet, a) it still could b) it almost definitely will in Coors. Of course the big risk here is that Welker won't get to enjoy such friendly confines given that there are about a half-dozen talented infielders ahead of him on the current depth chart. But even if Welker does change organizations, he's a potential top-15 fantasy third baseman in a neutral setting, and could fight his way into top-10 or -12 if he stays in Colorado. He's a top-101 guy for me, if only by a little.

**6** **Riley Pint  RHP**          OFP: BLANK   Likely: BLANK
ETA: 2021. There's a large SD here too though.
Born: 11/06/97   Age: 21   Bats: R   Throws: R   Height: 6'4"   Weight: 195
Origin: Round 1, 2016 Draft (#4 overall)

**The Report:** Ordinal team lists—really ordinal prospect rankings at all—to a certain extent are always going to be exercises in false precision. But some prospects are going to be more dart throws than others—Tommy John recoveries, third-round prep picks with upside, complex league guys (who might also be third-round prep picks with upside). Then there's Riley Pint. He was limited to just eight innings in 2018 due to a forearm injury. This followed a 2017 that was developmentally weird at best. The potential talent here is undeniable, but eventually the potential has to actualize. I can tell you that the Rockies are still saying all the right things publicly here, because of course they are. I can tell you there's still an elite fastball lurking in the profile. But we've now gone beyond unknown unknowns with Pint.

Now strictly speaking, Riley Pint is probably not the sixth best prospect in the Rockies system. He's maybe second or perhaps not on the list; there's your one standard deviation. But this feels close enough, nestled in a tier of his own between the safer major-league bets and the relievers and fourth outfielders. Prospect lists are a snapshot in time as my predecessor used to say. This report is an underdeveloped polaroid.

**The Risks:** Extreme. That one I can answer.

**Ben Carsley's Fantasy Take:** He's the arm I'd be most willing to gamble on in this system, but sometimes it's smarter to just walk away from the table.

**7** **Yency Almonte  RHP**          OFP: 55   Likely: 45   ETA: Debuted in 2018
Born: 06/04/94   Age: 25   Bats: B   Throws: R   Height: 6'3"   Weight: 205
Origin: Round 17, 2012 Draft (#537 overall)

**The Report:** I've always had a soft spot for Almonte. When I saw him in Hartford, he worked quickly, threw strikes, flashed a plus slider, and did a good job measuring out his stuff across his outings. He was usually good for keeping the game time under 2:45 so I could get down the road to the cocktail bar at a reasonable hour. So yeah, he was easy to like. I did think he was a reliever long term because of intermittent shoulder issues and the lack of an average changeup. The Rockies transitioned him to the pen full-time after a June call-up, and the early results were quite good.

As you'd expect with this kind of conversion, Almonte's velocity ticked up into the mid-90s, and he leaned more heavily on his mid-80s plus slider. Almonte manipulates the slider well and he's comfortable enough throwing it to the backfoot against lefties to make it a crossover weapon. The change is still below-average. It's very firm but flashes average run and sink. It's enough to keep it in the back of hitters' minds at least, but not much more than that. Health permitting, Almonte is a major-league-ready late-inning reliever, although a part of me wishes they gave him a little more time in the rotation outside of the launching pad in Albuquerque.

**The Risks:** Low. Almonte got a fair bit of major-league time, has two present above-average major league offerings, and has a chance to break camp in the Rockies bullpen.

**Ben Carsley's Fantasy Take:** I'm a bit bummed that the Rockies have transitioned Almonte to the pen, as I liked him a bit as a starter prospect. Alas, it's tough for us to get excited about *any* reliever prospects, nevermind ones who'll be pitching in Coors. Sadly, you can pass, though Almonte may be worthy of your watch list in super-deep formats or leagues with holds as a category.

### 8. Tyler Nevin   1B

OFP: 55   Likely: 45   ETA: 2020
Born: 05/29/97   Age: 22   Bats: R   Throws: R   Height: 6'4"   Weight: 200
Origin: Round 1, 2015 Draft (#38 overall)

**The Report:** Health has been a limiting factor for Nevin since he was knee-high to a baseball-playing grasshopper. But he finally showed flashes of what he's capable of with the bat last season. He wears the standard Lancaster caveat for last year's when-healthy production, but he attacks hittable pitches in the zone well and he can hit balls that'll get out of any stadium. He's built long, square, and powerful, and the swing stays fluid off a long stride into the attack. He sprayed balls all over the place in Arizona in a rousing fall campaign, and has at least enough physicality and arm strength to keep giving him reps at third base.

**The Risks:** They're high physically until they're not. His medical file's long and storied, though despite a couple short stints in the tent last season he did log 117 games. As it is for so many guys, Double-A presents a significant test here.

**Ben Carsley's Fantasy Take:** Nevin is a platoon guy/corner bench bat through and through for me. If he remains a Rockie, he's unlikely to play everyday. If he gets traded he could be a second-division starter, but then, well, he's not a Rockie. His offensive upside and proximity may be enough to sneak him on a top-200, but any rosier outlook right now relies too heavily on bloodlines.

### 9. Yonathan Daza   OF

OFP: 50   Likely: 40   ETA: Late 2019
Born: 02/28/94   Age: 25   Bats: R   Throws: R   Height: 6'2"   Weight: 190
Origin: International Free Agent, 2010

**The Report:** Daza was limited to just 54 games in Hartford this year because of a hamstring injury. Despite the rawness in his game, he acquitted himself well in his first taste of Double-A. He's a quick-twitch athlete, a plus runner who's a steady defender in center field, and he shows enough arm for right. His bat needs to take a step forward to get him over the hump from fourth outfielder to starter, though.

Daza's swing is loose—in a good way—with quick wrists. It's bat speed over barrel control at present. He has the raw physical tools for average hit, but struggles with spin and his general aggressiveness at the plate looks ripe for exploitation by major-league arms. There's enough strength and loft—he'll put a charge in a mistake—to project average power, but you wonder how much of that he will get into games against elite pitching. Daza turns 25 in February and seems ticketed for a return engagement with the Eastern League, so the clock is ticking on his development, and the Rockies already have a very crowded outfield picture.

**The Risks:** High. He's overaged, hasn't fully conquered Double-A, and there are hit tool questions.

**Ben Carsley's Fantasy Take:** There are worse bets than a toolsy outfielder who could challenge for playing time in Colorado this season, but Daza has enough red flags in his profile that I'm wary of going all-in here. Between the health issues, his age relative to competition and the glut of outfielders in front of him, Daza seems destined for a future as a fourth outfielder. Could he be of use for us if he ends up getting more playing time? Sure. But the odds of him starting everyday for the Rox seem pretty slim.

### 10

**Ryan Vilade SS**  OFP: 50  Likely: 40  ETA: 2021
Born: 02/18/99  Age: 20  Bats: R  Throws: R  Height: 6'2"  Weight: 194
Origin: Round 2, 2017 Draft (#48 overall)

**The Report:** The Rockies second-round prep pick in 2017, Vilade drew a somewhat aggressive A-ball assignment in his first full pro season. He held his own against generally older competition—albeit while playing his home games in one of the better hitter's parks in the minors. Drafted as a power over hit third baseman, Vilade played every game in the field this year at shortstop. He's "okay" there, but likely will slide back to third at some point in his pro career where the range and actions will play better. The arm is fine for either spot on the left side though.

At the plate, Vilade has plus bat speed, but works with an upper-body heavy swing that doesn't always keep him in balance or allow him to tap into his plus raw power. He's got enough hand-eye to make consistent contact at this level, but without further refinement both the quality and amount of contact might go down by the upper minors. He's athletic, projectable, and you usually can't teach this kind of bat speed. Ultimately, there's a foundation worth betting on here. even if the upside might not be much beyond "major-league starter" unless the power takes a big step forward.

**The Risks:** High. May have to shift off shortstop and only an A-ball track record.

**Ben Carsley's Fantasy Take:** I think it's fair to say that Vilade's upside appears much lower today than it did when he was drafted. Does an average-ish third baseman who plays half of his games in Coors Field have fantasy value? You betcha. But considering that's Vilade's upside, he'd likely be toward the end of a top-200 list and nothing more.

## The Next Five:

### 11  Grant Lavigne   1B
Born: 08/27/99   Age: 19   Bats: L   Throws: R   Height: 6'4"   Weight: 220
Origin: Round 1, 2018 Draft (#42 overall)

Our image of the prep first baseman usually fits in one of two molds. (1) The advanced hitters with fringe athleticism who may or may not add enough game power as they move up the totem pole (Dominic Smith or Nick Pratto). (2) The leveraged slugger with even fringier athleticism and usually significant hit tool questions (Josh Ockimey or Bobby Bradley). Lavigne threads the needle here. He's a strong kid with a reasonably athletic frame that doesn't need to get too long or too leveraged to tap into his substantial raw power. There's the beginnings of a quality approach here as well, with more polish than you'd expect from a cold-weather high school bat.

The main quibble is that, well, he's still a first baseman. Lavigne may not be your *average* prep first base pick, but the bar for major-league performance is still as high as every other cold corner prospect. And the hit or pop alone might not be a carrying tool, so he will still have to prove it level-by-level.

### 12  Justin Lawrence   RHP
Born: 11/25/94   Age: 24   Bats: R   Throws: R   Height: 6'3"   Weight: 220
Origin: Round 12, 2015 Draft (#347 overall)

Lawrence got beat in a couple high-profile prospect showcases and ran out of steam a bit by Arizona, but he was absolutely disgusting for most of the year. At his peak he threw a nice stretch of innings in the Antelope Valley summertime elements. He sits in the high-90s with a darting, two-plane slider a dozen mph slower, all out of a twisting, slingshotting delivery that creates a real tough pick-up for righties and a pretty difficult one for lefties too. It was unclear to the naked eye why he never graduated to Hartford last season, but if he brings that stuff with him when he does, he'll force his way into Colorado's bullpen development plan this season.

### 13  Ben Bowden   LHP
Born: 10/21/94   Age: 24   Bats: L   Throws: L   Height: 6'4"   Weight: 235
Origin: Round 2, 2016 Draft (#45 overall)

**14**    **Robert Tyler   RHP**
Born: 06/18/95   Age: 24   Bats: R   Throws: R   Height: 6'4"   Weight: 226
Origin: Round 1, 2016 Draft (#38 overall)

These two are a package deal. They've travelled a bizarrely exact path—they were drafted seven picks apart, both missed 2017 recuperating from Tommy John, and they've climbed Colorado's minor league ladder nearly in lockstep—and each should get their chances at Double-A this year. Both have fast-track potential if they show well when they do. Tyler was gassed at the end of the season, while Bowden held up better and flashed a slightly higher-end ceiling. Tyler throws a bit harder and Bowden offers a quality pitch mix from the left side. Neither looks like a budding relief ace but they could both wind up as valuable bullpen contributors.

**15**    **Rico Garcia   RHP**
Born: 01/10/94   Age: 25   Bats: R   Throws: R   Height: 5'11"   Weight: 190
Origin: Round 30, 2016 Draft (#890 overall)

Garcia reached Double-A in 2018, closing out a very productive season for the Hawaii product. There is minimal projection left for Garcia, but he's effective filling up the zone with three averageish offerings. The fastball sits low-90s (although he has flashed higher at times) and features some sink and run from his high-three-quarters slot. His slider is pinned around 80. While it lacks consistent shape, the best are solid-average with late, tight bite. The changeup is on the fringier side of average and is a clear third pitch. Garcia is a shorter, overaged righty, but the present stuff is good enough for a backend starter or swing projection, with a middle relief fallback if he finds more velo in shorter bursts.

## Others of note:

### Sam Hilliard, OF, Double-A Hartford

Hilliard falls along the Tauchmann/Patterson continuum of fringy Rockies corner prospects. He's not a precise fit for this type. He's sneaky athletic, an average runner who's a good glove/plus arm in right and could probably even stand in center for you once a week. It is still a corner outfield profile though, and the bat may not carry it.

The power is on point. It's plus raw and Hilliard will absolutely punish mistakes, but the stiffness in his swing and pitch recognition issues limited how much of that raw got into games against Double-A arms. Hilliard also has platoon issues, and it's fair to mention that he benefited from Hartford's short porch in right. He will be 25 before Opening Day. He straddles the bench outfielder/org guy line for now, but I always liked Jordan Patterson more than most too.

### Ryan Castellani, OF, Double-A Hartford

Castellani entered the 2018 season as the fifth best prospect in the Colorado system and a long-list 101 guy. I ended up seeing him four times in 2017 the way the schedule shook out and saw a slightly different dude each time. He was extremely young for Double-A though. You could easily imagine a scenario where he put it together in a second look at the Eastern League and beat a path to the majors as another homegrown arm in a suddenly rich Rockies pipeline. Instead, his age-22 season in Double-A went far worse than his age-21 campaign.

The vagaries of the schedule meant I didn't catch Castellani until the last couple weeks of the season, but he again looked like a different pitcher, in not in a good way. His slot was higher, his arm action more rigid. Gone was the athletic delivery that garnered physical comps to Max Scherzer. There was more effort to sit 89-91, the slider was slurvier, and he just didn't look right. You'd catch glimpses of the 2017 top prospect—a fastball that bored in under a lefty's hands, a mid-80s slider with late tilt, but if you only saw him last year, you wouldn't be filing him as an acquire. Twenty-three in Double-A, even as a double repeater, isn't a prospect death sentence. But pitchers, man.

## Top Talents 25 and Under (born 4/1/93 or later):

1. German Marquez
2. Kyle Freeland
3. Brendan Rodgers
4. David Dahl
5. Garrett Hampson
6. Ryan McMahon
7. Raimel Tapia
8. Trevor Story
9. Ryan Rolison
10. Antonio Senzatela
11. Peter Lambert

Trevor Story aged off of this list just in the nick of time to avoid launching the whole exercise into the sun, and yet even with that kind of heavyweight graduation, this is still one of the best batches of young talent this franchise has ever accumulated.

The dual emergence of Marquez and Freeland last year was a sight for the sorest of pitching-shriveled eyes, especially as former staple of this list Jon Gray staggered throughout the year. Marquez really honed his raw talent quickly over the last year, developing one of the filthiest Kershaw mixes since, well, Kershaw. Freeland threw the ball well all year, then added a couple ticks to his cutter and took his game to the next level down the stretch. The Rockies have never started a season with as much reason for optimism about their starting pitching, and both guys are under club control for the next four years.

Dahl just balled once he got rolling in Coors. His raw talent has long been obvious, but he's missed so much time and spent so much recovery effort on the shelf over the years that he's long been a bit of a wild card. There were a few ugly indicators about his approach all year, but he just kept right on crushing the ball. He's always been a talented player; here's hoping we see what it looks like for a full season.

McMahon's hit well in a bunch of runs against Triple-A pitching now, and the club gave him 200 trips between two demotions to show them what he could do in Denver last year. Then he ended up riding pine for nearly all of September and Rocktober. The Daniel Murphy signing clouds his short-term outlook all the more, but he is currently a talented, versatile young infielder with some potential.

Tapia put up a modestly above-average offensive season when controlled for Albuquerque's shenanigans, but it was chock-full of the kind of doubles and triples with eyes he should be able to spray all around Coors Field. He'll be 25 on Opening Day and really needs to get some at-bats.

Senzatela was able to work pretty effectively last year off a fastball-slider-curve three-piece, then brought in the ol' number four wiggle down the stretch, coaxing a nice boost in whiff rate when he did. He'll have an interesting multi-inning swing profile for as long as the fastball holds.

# Part 3: Featured Articles

# The Hole in The Shift is Fixing Itself

## Russell Carleton

**I**'ve been on a bit of a mission against The Shift of late. I'm not out to get The Shift for the usual reasons that people oppose it. The words "the right way to play the game" won't be found on my lips. If a team wants to pursue a strategy that is within the rules and it works, then by all means, they have my blessing (not that they need it). Instead, my concern with The Shift is a worry that it doesn't work, or at least that it has a flaw that needs fixing.

The data show that while The Shift does a decent job of preventing singles on balls in play (what it's supposed to do), it also increases the number of walks that happen in front of it, and the number of additional walks outweighs the number of singles saved. It's a problem because you can't throw a guy out if he gets to walk to first base.

But the "why" was important. It seemed that The Shift was changing the way in which pitchers pitched. We saw that there were fewer fastballs thrown in front of The Shift than we might otherwise expect, and that pitchers tended to stay out of the strike zone a little more. Not by a lot. In fact, it might not even be visible to the naked eye. The percentage of pitches that are out of the zone goes from 51.0 to 53.3 from a standard defense (two right/two left) to a full shift (three on one side). That difference stands up even after we control for the types of hitters that get shifted against. And it's enough to drive up the walk rate to where it cancels out the benefits that teams thought they were getting with The Shift… and then some.

But there was some hope. I found that when individual pitchers stayed closer to the in-zone/out-of-zone mix that they used without The Shift on, they could still get the benefits of The Shift without the walk problems. So, in theory, a team could simply figure out a way to convince its pitchers to not fall prey to the walk trap and The Shift would once again be their friend.

It's reasonable to think that some teams might be more hip to this idea than others. Maybe some figured it out a year before the others. Maybe they were better at getting the message across to their pitchers. Or, maybe no one has figured it out yet.

**Warning! Gory Mathematical Details Ahead!**

# Colorado Rockies 2019

I used data from 2015-2017, made available through MLB's data portal, Baseball Savant. They are kind enough to note when teams are using an infield shift (three fielders on one side of second base), as opposed to a "strategic shift" (someone's playing a bit out of position, but it's not quite that drastic) or a "standard" alignment.

Since we're doing this by team, I can't just look at raw walk rates, because we know that some teams have good pitchers and others have not-so-good pitchers. Some have a mix of both. I used the log-odds ratio method to take into account a batter's general walking proclivities, and a pitcher's as well, and then shoving them into a binary logistic regression. Then, I asked the computer to generate a specific coefficient for each team's pitchers, for when they went into The Shift and how that affected their walk rate.

Using those coefficients, I was able to project what would happen if a league-average pitcher faced a league-average hitter (which we expect would product a league-average walk rate; from 2015-2017, 7.7 percent of plate appearances ended in a walk) and then just switched his hat. Here's the top five and the bottom five:

| Top 5 Teams | Projected Shift Walk Rate | Bottom 5 Teams | Projected Shift Walk Rate |
|---|---|---|---|
| Rockies | 6.2% | Rangers | 11.2% |
| Pirates | 6.7% | Mets | 10.4% |
| Indians | 7.2% | Dodgers | 10.2% |
| Astros | 7.3% | Cardinals | 9.9% |
| Braves | 7.7% | Tigers | 9.7% |

There are probably people out there right now trying to figure out what the common thread is among the top and bottom teams. I'm sure, because this is Baseball Prospectus, people are already trying to make the case that sabermetric "early adopters" have some sort of edge here. I think that the more interesting piece is that by the time you get to fifth place in The Shift, we're at league average.

As a sanity check, I examined the issue on a pitch-by-pitch level, looking at how often pitchers threw their pitches in the GameDay strike zone, and again using the same basic methodology and getting team-specific coefficients. The names on the list re-arranged themselves, but the idea was the same, and the two lists correlated with an R of .593.

There's a reason that I don't usually do this type of leaderboard post. I don't really know what the Rockies, Pirates, Indians, Astros, and Braves have in common, or what they have that the bottom five don't. I can put a shrug emoji here and say, "Well, it must be something!" but that seems like a cop-out. Instead, I'd like to present another table and suggest that the table above doesn't even really matter anymore.

| Year | League Percent Outside K Zone (Full Shift) | League Percent in K Zone (No Shift) | Difference |
|---|---|---|---|
| 2015 | 54.1% | 51.1% | 3.0% |
| 2016 | 53.3% | 50.9% | 2.4% |
| 2017 | 52.6% | 50.9% | 1.7% |
| 2018 | 52.0% | 50.7% | 1.3% |

The hole in The Shift is fixing itself, and it's coming down really fast league wide. In my earlier work on The Shift, I suggested that until teams stopped having such a huge difference between their out-of-zone rate with and without The Shift on, there would just be too many walks for The Shift to make sense. It seems that all 30 of them have been working toward just that. I once estimated that it takes about 10 years for an idea to filter its way through baseball. At this rate, it looks like teams are going to catch up a lot faster than that. And yeah, they're all saber-smart now.

It's likely that whatever magic it was that the Rockies and Pirates had has made its way to Texas and Queens. Or is at least on its way. And if teams are committing to fixing the walk problem, then it's likely that they will continue shifting and shifting a lot.

And eventually it's going to actually make sense for them to do it.

—*Russell Carleton is a former author of Baseball Prospectus and now an analyst for the New York Mets.*

# The State of the Quality Start

## Rob Mains

One of the seven things you (probably) didn't know about the 2018 season is that quality starts—defined as a start lasting six or more innings with three or fewer earned runs allowed—as a percentage of total starts cratered to an all-time low of 41 percent. I want to look a little more deeply into this, since it's been a while (May of 2016, to be exact) since I've examined quality starts.

The term *quality start* is credited to *Philadelphia Inquirer* sportswriter John Lowe. It's been derided ever since he coined it in December of 1985. Three runs in six innings? That's a 4.50 ERA! In what world is that a measure of quality?

Let's start with that criticism. It's true that 3 x 9 / 6 = 4.5. (You came here for this sort of high-level math, right?) But it's also true that type of start, meeting the bare minimum for earning a quality start, is unusual. Here's the proportion of quality starts in which the pitcher lasted exactly six innings and yielded exactly three earned runs. (I'm going to confine this analysis to the 30-team era, 1998-present. Almost all data retrieved in this article is via the Baseball-Reference Play Index.)

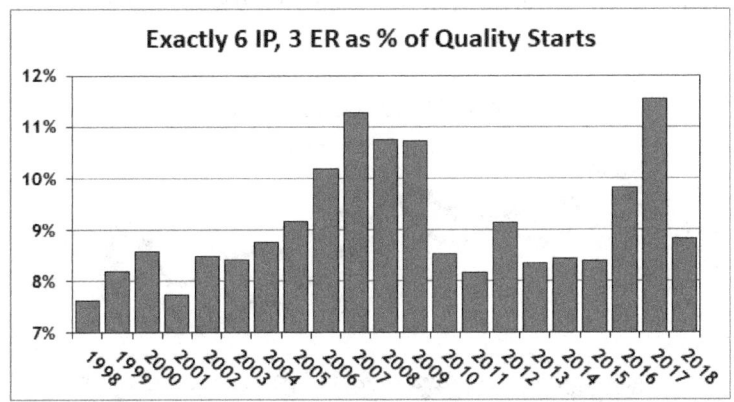

There were 1,997 quality starts in 2018. Only 176, or fewer than one in 11, featured a pitcher going six innings and allowing three earned runs. Put another way, the percentage of quality starts that resulted in a 4.50 ERA (8.8 percent) is less than half the percentage of games in which a batter hit two home runs and his team lost (22.5 percent; 237-69 won-lost). That doesn't impugn hitting two homers.

So if a 4.50 ERA isn't the norm, what is? How good are quality starts?

Pretty good, it turns out. First, on a team level:

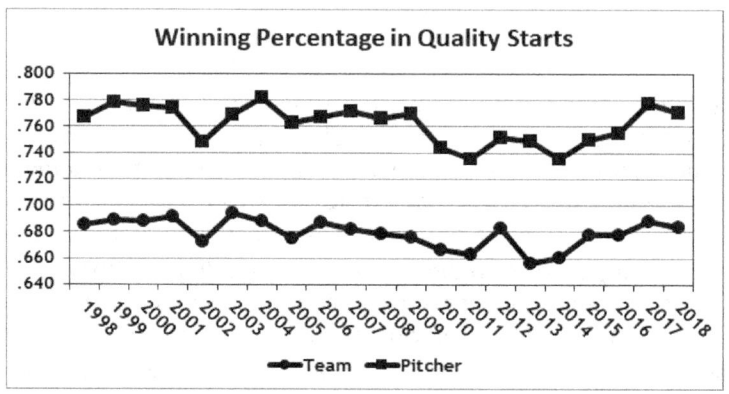

Teams receiving a quality start from their pitcher won 68.4 percent of their games in 2018, in line with the 30-team era average of 67.9 percent. A team with a .684 winning percentage wins 111 games. Getting a quality start is definitely a good thing. Individual pitchers throwing quality starts have a higher winning percentage because a big slice of team losses is assigned to a reliever.

If teams do well in quality starts, how well do the starting pitchers do? Again, very well.

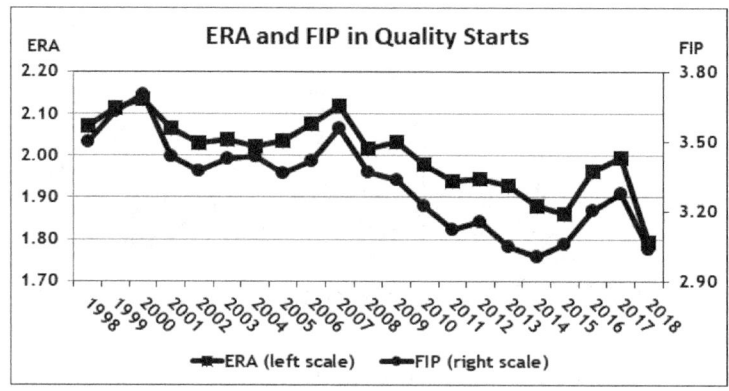

Pitchers in quality starts had a 1.79 ERA (blue line) in 2018, *the lowest in the 30-team era*. Their FIP was higher, 3.04, but still excellent. In the 30-team era, only 2014 had a lower FIP for quality starts, 3.01.

But, of course, the run environment in 2014 was different. Teams in 2014 scored 4.07 runs per game, the fewest in a non-strike year since 1976. They scored 4.45 runs per game in 2018. So surrendering a 3.04 FIP in 2018 is more impressive than 3.01 in 2014. Accordingly, let's look at ERA and FIP in quality starts relative to league averages.

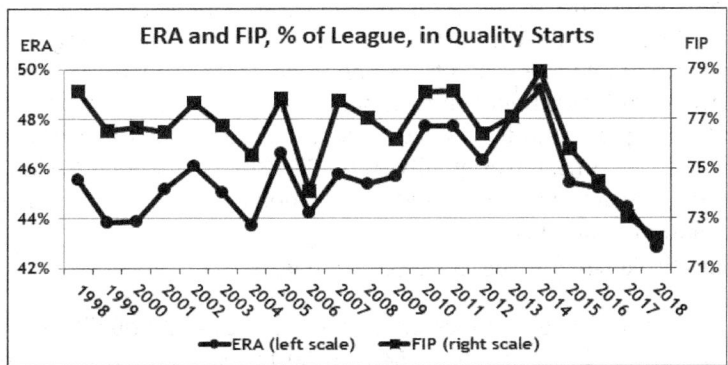

This tells a more dramatic story. Starting pitchers in 2018 gave up a 4.19 ERA and a 4.21 FIP. Starters in quality starts gave up a 1.79 ERA, 43 percent of the league average. Starters in quality starts gave up a 3.04 FIP, 72 percent of the league average. Both of these marks represent lows in the 30-team era.

The takeaway here is this: *Quality starts are better, relative to other starts, than they've ever been over the past 21 years.*

Maybe during the winter I'll look at this over a longer arc of time. For now, though, we can definitively say quality starts are the best they've ever been since the Diamondbacks and Rays joined the majors.

Yet, paradoxically, they're down.

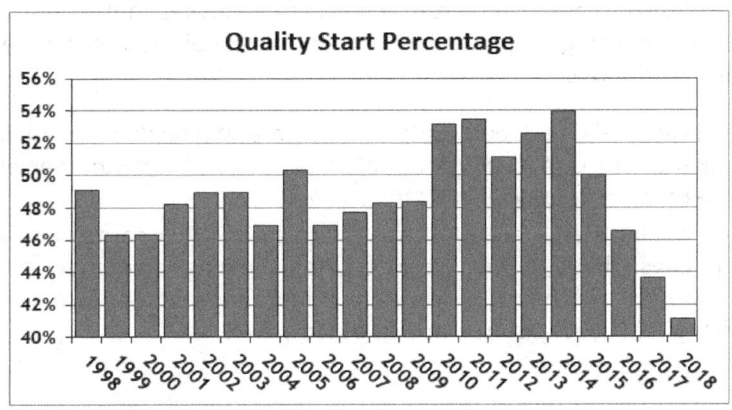

This graph covers only the 30-team era. In my article last week, though, I looked at the years 1908-2018. The result was the same. The 41 percent of starts in 2018 that were quality starts are an all-time low, well below the runners-up: 1930's 43 percent (the year teams scored an all-time record 5.55 runs per game) and last year's 44 percent.

The normal explanation for a dip in quality start percentage is an increase in scoring. When teams score a lot of runs, it's harder for starting pitchers to last six or more innings and limit opponents to three earned runs. From 1998 to 2014, the correlation between runs scored per game and the percentage of starts that were quality starts was -0.94. That means there was an extremely close relationship: More runs, fewer quality starts. Too small a sample? Go back to the start of the Expansion Era, 1961, and the relationship is even more negative, a -0.95 correlation, though 2014.

But that's broken down over the past four years:

- 2015: Runs per game increased from 4.07 to 4.25, quality start percentage decreased from 54.0 to 50.1. Yes, that's a negative relationship, but the regression model would predict a decline of 1.5 percentage points. We got 3.9 instead.
- 2016: Runs per game increased from 4.25 to 4.48, quality start percentage decreased from 50.1 to 46.6. Past experience would suggest a decline of just 1.8 percentage points. We got 3.4.
- 2017: Runs per game increased from 4.48 to 4.65, quality start percentage decreased from 46.6 to 43.6. Again, the direction's right, but the magnitude isn't. Using the relationship from 1998 to 2014, that increase in scoring should've reduced quality starts by 1.3 percentage points, not 2.9.
- 2018: Runs per game declined from 4.65 to 4.45. That should've resulted in the quality start percentage moving in the other direction, rising 1.6 points. It didn't. It fell 2.6 points, as noted, to an all-time low.

Granted, we're talking about just four years here. Maybe they're outliers. But I don't think they are. Quality starts, as noted, are as good or better than ever. But they're rarer than ever as well. And I think I know why.

To get a quality start, you need to allow three or fewer earned and pitch at least six innings. That's 18 outs. Here's a graph showing the number of starting pitchers who limited their opponents to three or fewer earned runs but got pulled after pitching at least five innings but fewer than six:

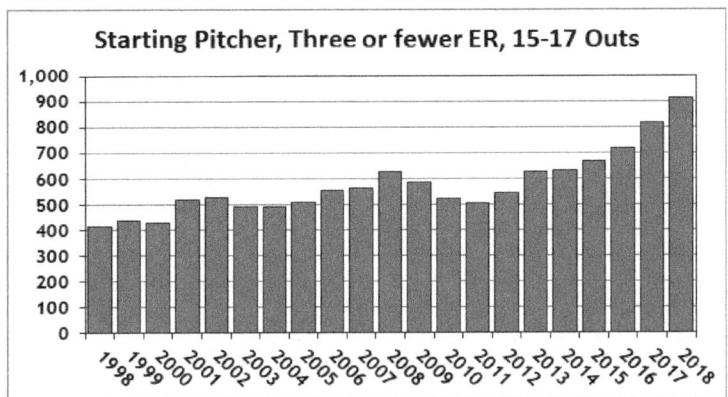

A pitcher getting 15 outs pitched five innings. A pitcher getting 16 outs pitched 5 1/3. A pitcher getting 17 outs pitched 5 2/3. More than ever before, pitchers are being removed from games in which they are within 1-3 outs of a quality start, falling just short of the six-inning finish line. Widespread acknowledgement of the times-through-the-order penalty and a flotilla of available bullpen arms is making the quality start simultaneously both more excellent and more rare.

Which is ironic, given that we saw a new post-war quality start record this season:

| Rank | Pitcher | Season | Consecutive QS |
|---|---|---|---|
| 1 | Jacob deGrom | 2018 | 24 |
| 2 | Bob Gibson | 1968 | 22 |
| - | Chris Carpenter | 2005 | 22 |
| 4 | Johan Santana | 2004 | 21 |
| 5 | Luis Tiant | 1968 | 20 |
| - | Mike Scott | 1986 | 20 |
| - | Jake Arrieta | 2015 | 20 |
| 8 | Robin Roberts | 1952 | 19 |
| - | Tom Seaver | 1973 | 19 |
| - | Jack Morris | 1983 | 19 |
| - | Greg Maddux | 1998 | 19 |
| - | Josh Johnson | 2010 | 19 |
| - | Jon Lester | 2014 | 19 |

While there have been longer streaks spread over multiple seasons, no pitcher since World War II threw more consecutive quality starts in one year than Jacob deGrom this year. The fact that he did in a year in which quality starts were the rarest they've ever been adds to the accomplishment.

*—Rob Mains is an author of Baseball Prospectus.*

# Heads-Up Hacking—The First Pitch

## Matthew Trueblood

**B**atters fell behind in a higher percentage of all plate appearances in 2018 than in any previous season for which we have pitch-by-pitch data. That kind of granular information goes back only to 1988, but we might safely assume (given all we know about baseball as it had been before that, and as it has been in the years since) that batters have *never* fallen behind at a higher rate than they did last season.

Through the 1990s, the percentage of all plate appearances that began 0-1 hovered in the high 30s and low 40s. In the 2000s, it rose steadily but slowly, through the mid-40s. In 2018, 49.8 percent of all trips to the plate began 0-1. That, as much as anything, captures in microcosm the nature of hitting in MLB today.

A countdown clock toward strike three begins ticking almost the moment a batter takes his place in the box. The league's adjusted OPS+ on the first pitch was higher in 2018 than ever before, and that has been true in most of the last 10 seasons. Batters hit .264/.289/.442 in all plate appearances in which they swung at the first pitch last season, and .241/.330/.395 in all plate appearances in which they took that first offering.

The percentage differences in batting average and isolated power there favor swinging at the first pitch by more than in any season since 1988, while the difference in on-base percentage favors taking by more than ever. If you want to get on base at a decent clip, it's a good idea to be patient, but you run the risk of missing the only chances you'll get to produce power.

## Colorado Rockies 2019

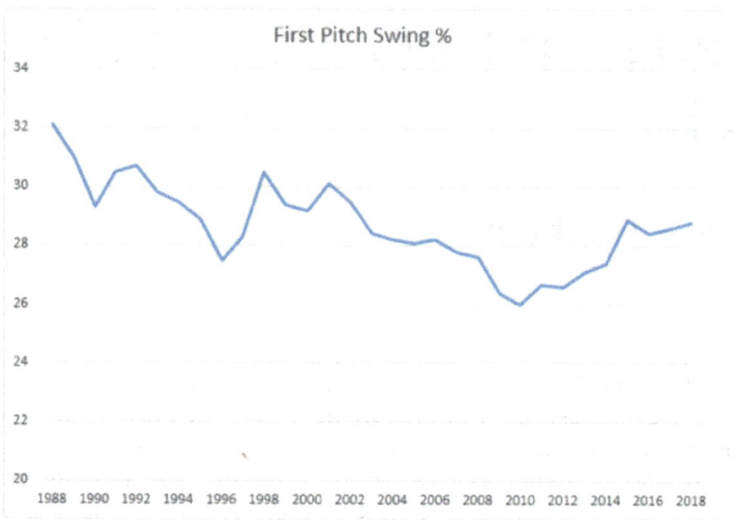

The league swung at the first pitch 28.8 percent of the time in 2018. With the isolated exception of 2015, that's the highest that number has climbed since 2002, but it might not be high enough. With the help of BP research maven Rob McQuown, I looked at the aggregate Called Strike Probability (CSProb) on the first pitch for each season since 2008, when the implementation of PITCHf/x first made measuring that possible. It's risen sharply during that period.

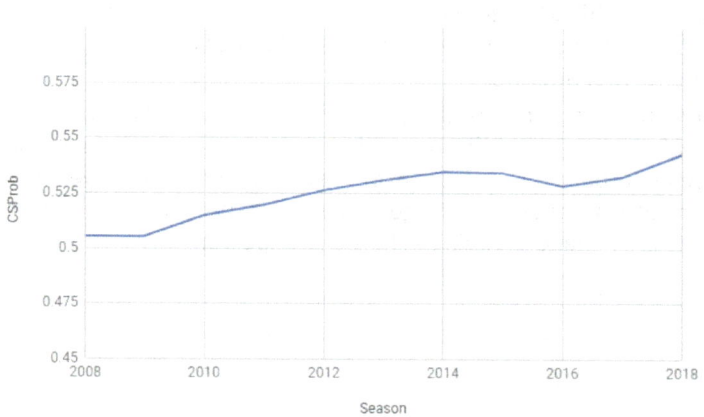

*Called Strike Probability, First Pitch of PA (2008-2018)*

Called Strike Probability is exactly what it sounds like: a pitch with a given CSProb has roughly that chance of being called a strike, if not swung at. In 2018, a batter who took 100 first pitches from a random sampling of the league's pitchers might expect to fall behind 54 or 55 times—up from 50 or 51 times in 2008. Almost regardless of pitch type (and, notably, especially in the case of fastballs), the first pitch tends to have more of the zone right now than ever before.

Pitchers are better at throwing strikes. They have better stuff, and believe more in their ability to miss bats within the zone. Perhaps most importantly, they know that batters are looking for one thing on the first pitch: a fastball. If they don't get it, they're likely to take the pitch. Check out how the use of sinkers and four-seamers on the first pitch has changed in a decade:

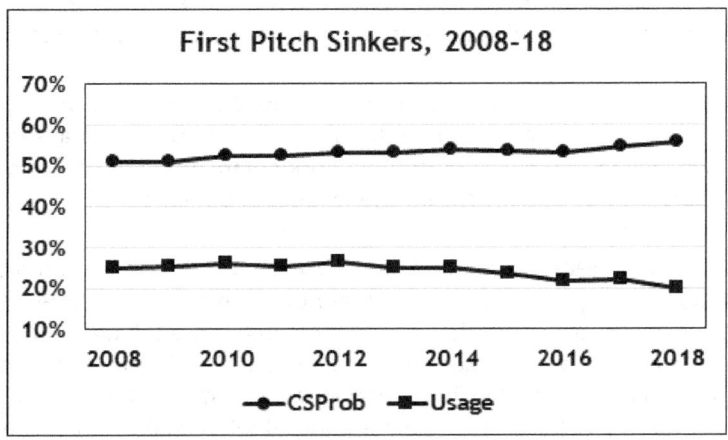

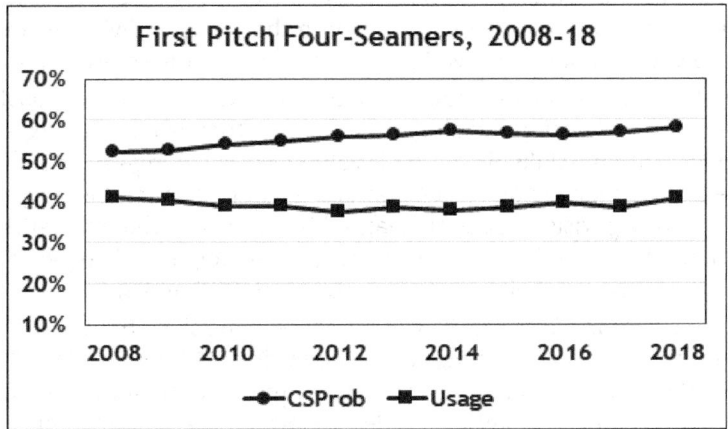

The sinker is losing its place in baseball, but the rate at which pitchers have thrown it on the first pitch hasn't dropped any faster than its usage rate in other counts. Pitchers have actually gone to their four-seamer *more* often to open counts, in the last few years, after a dip in the 2012-2015 period. What's really changed, though, and what shows up in both charts above, is that pitchers are catching more of the zone with first-pitch fastballs than they were a decade ago, or a half-decade ago. They're attacking right away, even with the pitch they know batters are expecting. The message is pretty clear: batters are being too passive.

Sliders, curves, and changeups each have more of the zone when thrown on the first pitch than they did several years ago, too, though the effect is less pronounced. Pitchers have seen the numbers; they know batters are doing better on the first pitch itself. They still feel safe throwing more and better strikes than ever before, figuring they'll come out ahead as long as they keep getting ahead to open each battle.

The Moneyball revolution brought an increased league-wide focus on OBP, which resulted in a de facto mandate to take a more patient tack at the plate. It worked very well for a while, as batters with poor plate discipline were compelled to either adjust or be expelled from the league, and pitchers with poor control were slowly weeded out.

However, concurrent with that revolution, and spurred by it in some ways, was the evolution of the pitching paradigm that now dominates the game. As batters ratcheted up their focus on inflating pitch counts and working walks, pitchers honed theirs on throwing strikes and missing bats. The league's understanding of what makes a good pitcher improved at least as much, from the mid-1990s through the mid-2000s, as its understanding of what makes a good hitter. As amphetamines and other performance-enhancing drugs were phased mostly out of the game, and as PITCHf/x broke onto the scene, individuals and teams learned how to exploit the evolved approaches of even the smartest hitters.

The ability to avoid making outs is still the most valuable one in baseball, but the magnitude of its eclipse of slugging is smaller than ever. To a greater extent than power, on-base skills derive their value from chaining—from the on-base skill levels of the players on either side of a given individual. Eleven years ago, when the housing crisis hit, people learned the hard way that the value of their homes depended a good deal on the values of their neighbors' homes. The same wasn't true, though, of their cars. So it is now, with OBP and SLG.

The global OBP in 2018 was .318. The only seasons since the Dead Ball Era in which the league got on base at a worse clip were 2013-2015, 1988, 1971-1972, and 1963-1968. This is all happening despite the aforementioned evolution of the science of hitting. It's happening despite a shift in approach and focus, one that would steer OBP ever higher, if only it were working.

Instead, it's sitting at a low ebb, and while it does so, even guys who get on base often are a little less helpful than they were 10 years ago—or 20, or 40, or 60, or 70, or 80, or 90. They're less helpful, that is, because unless there happen to be three or four other guys in the lineup who get on just as regularly, their contribution is merely to forestall the inevitable. Runs happen, increasingly, when a sudden bang happens, and that means attacking early in the count—because pitchers are sure as hell doing that.

In a league making contact on barely 75 percent of its swings, and a league in which an increasing number of pitchers can throw multiple off-speed pitches for strikes in any count, the only way to consistently generate offense is going to be aggressive. This isn't necessarily true for individuals, like Mookie Betts and Jose Ramirez, who make a lot of contact and have excellent plate discipline, and whose power comes from such natural quickness in a short stroke. Most players have to make tradeoffs, though, whether it be lowering their contact rate or raising their chase rate, in order to consistently make the quality of contact necessary to survive in today's game.

| Highest % | Lowest % |
|---|---|
| Javier Baez – 48.3 | Joe Mauer – 4.6 |
| Freddie Freeman – 47.1 | Mookie Betts – 9.7 |
| Ozzie Albies – 46.3 | Brett Gardner – 10.7 |
| Jose Altuve – 44.2 | Jose Ramirez – 12.0 |
| Nick Castellanos – 44.1 | Jason Kipnis – 13.8 |
| Joey Gallo – 42.3 | Jesus Aguilar – 14.5 |
| Corey Dickerson – 40.9 | Xander Bogaerts – 15.8 |
| Salvador Perez – 40.8 | Brian Dozier – 16.3 |
| Eddie Rosario – 40.7 | Mike Trout – 17.6 |
| Nick Ahmed – 40.4 | Yasmani Grandal – 17.6 |

*Top 10 and Bottom 10 Hitters, First-Pitch Swing Rate (2018)*

The question isn't which of these lists one prefers, but what they each convey, qualitatively, about the cat-and-mouse game of early-count hitting. Those top five on the left, especially, drive home the fact that for most players, getting aggressive early in the count is now key to keeping strikeout rate down and hitting for power.

For now, the message is: pitchers are coming right after batters with the nastiest stuff they've ever had. Batters had better stop giving away strike one and force hurlers to adjust, or the global OBP crisis is only going to get worse. ∎

—*Matthew Trueblood is an author of Baseball Prospectus.*

# A Hymn for the Index Stat

## Patrick Dubuque

We survived without computers. I know this, because I remember the day when my dad hooked up his brand-new Atari 400 computer to the back of our 12-inch Magnavox television, and the perfect blue of the memo pad lit up for the first time. I was born just on the edge of that transitional generation, of learning cursive and balancing checkbooks and just doing math all the time, constant manual arithmetic.

It still amazes me. We learned how to sail ships without computers. We learned how to do calculus. We built towers that didn't fall down, most of the time. We engineered catapults to knock them down anyway. We built a robust system of philosophy called "utilitarianism," founded on the principle that the good of an action is evaluated by summing the effects of that action, which is the kind of formula that would make the world's mainframes crash. The whole foundation of statistics as a field is "here's math you could easily do but would die of old age first."

The fact of the matter is that there is too much math in the world to do. There are too many things changing, and too many things too small to notice, for us to handle. At some point, they become too much for the computers to handle as well, which is why we have chaos theory and undetectable earthquakes, but it's not an even fight. At some point, we fall back on intuition, and given how under-equipped we are, we're forced to bestow that intuition with some sort of supernatural superiority, the "gut feeling," that we can't prove because we can only intuit that our intuition is better.

We're all lousy at intuition, and wonderful at lying to ourselves about it. The honest truth is that computers are far better at intuition than we are, because in order to know what feels "off" you have to know what's "on." In order to do that you have to constantly reassess the average of everything, then re-rank your own experience against it.

Test your own, by comparing these three anonymous lines:

| Player | G | HR | AVG | OBP | SLG |
|---|---|---|---|---|---|
| Player A | 156 | 38 | .259 | .342 | .535 |
| Player B | 154 | 38 | .280 | .348 | .527 |
| Player C | 158 | 38 | .266 | .343 | .509 |

These all seem like pretty similar players, right? The second one a touch more batted-ball dependent, the third a little less strong, but all pretty good hitters. And you'd be right, about the latter. Not the former.

Here's the breakdown:

- Player A: 1991 Howard Johnson, 141 DRC+
- Player B: 1996 Dean Palmer, 121 DRC+
- Player C: 2018 Giancarlo Stanton, 114 DRC+

Baseball is fortunate to have escaped the seismic shifts of so many other sports, where the talents and performances of other eras are nearly unrecognizable. (And not just other sports: try to explain the greatness of the movie Duck Soup without adjusting for era.) But they're still there, and they're nearly impossible to account for manually, without having to resort to sweeping generalizations like "steroid era" or juiced-ball era" to throw out entire swathes of production.

This is all to say that we should celebrate the index stat, that simple 100-based scale with such a humble aim: just to give context. It's hard to imagine how we lived without them for so long. Sabermetricians have always tried to make their stats look like other stats: True Average mapped to batting average, FIP molded to look like and compare to ERA. It's easy to understand the motivation—these statistics carry an emotional value in them that is hard to resist, as with the .300 hitter and the 2.00 ERA—but even they fall prey to the same loss of scale as their unadjusted counterparts. If a .300 average means different things in different years, does that hold true for a .300 True Average?

Instead, 100 doesn't say anything, except above average or below. And it does it instantly, for every season in every run environment for any statistic we want it to. We should have more index stats: K%+, so we can stop comparing Mike Clevinger's career 9.46 K/9 to Nolan Ryan's 9.55. HBP%+, so we can note that Ron Hunt was getting plunked when nobody else was getting plunked, as opposed to that imitator Brandon Guyer. Some might note how stale these references are and accuse league-adjustment as a backward-looking drive, and this is true. But we're always looking backward, always comparing the new with the expectations already set. The index stat just forces us to be honest.

There's always resistance to a new statistic, especially one so outwardly simple and so internally complex. We tend to stick with what we know, even in the case of formulas that are supposed to tell us what we know. But if your resistance is that it seems too complicated, too counterintuitive, too "black boxy," I encourage you to consider why you feel that way. Because the real world is infinitely more complicated than baseball, where all the pitches go in one basic direction and the baserunners are only allowed to travel in four directions. Baseball statistics based on mixed methodology are almost impossibly intricate. So are skyscrapers and automobiles. That's why we have computers—to take the guesswork out of them.

—*Patrick Dubuque is an author of Baseball Prospectus.*

# Index of Names

Abreu, Willie .................... 89
Almonte, Yency .............. 44, 97
Anderson, Tyler .................. 46
Arenado, Nolan .................. 18
Bettis, Chad ..................... 48
Blackmon, Charlie ............... 20
Bowden, Ben ............... 83, 100
Castellani, Ryan ........... 84, 101
Cuevas, Noel .................... 89
Dahl, David ..................... 22
Davis, Wade ..................... 50
Daza, Yonathan ............. 89, 98
Desmond, Ian .................... 24
Diaz, Eddy ...................... 89
Dunn, Mike ...................... 52
Estevez, Carlos ................. 90
Fernandez, Vince ................ 89
Freeland, Kyle .................. 54
Fuentes, Josh ................... 89
Garcia, Rico ............... 90, 101
Gonzalez, Rayan ................. 90
Gray, Jon ....................... 56
Hampson, Garrett ........... 76, 94
Hilliard, Sam .............. 77, 101
Hoffman, Jeff ................... 58
Howard, Sam ..................... 90
Humphreys, Reid ................. 90
Iannetta, Chris ................. 26
Johnson, D.J. ................... 85
Lambert, Peter .............. 86, 95
Lavigne, Grant ............. 78, 100
Lawrence, Justin ........... 90, 100
Marquez, German ................. 60
McGee, Jake ..................... 62
McMahon, Ryan ................... 28
Montano, Daniel ................. 89
Mundell, Brian .................. 89
Murphy, Daniel .................. 30
Murphy, Tom ..................... 32
Musgrave, Harrison .............. 64
Nevin, Tyler ................ 89, 98
Nikorak, Mike ................... 90
Nunez, Dom ...................... 89
Oberg, Scott .................... 66
Oh, Seung Hwan .................. 68
Pint, Riley ................. 87, 97
Ramos, Roberto .................. 89
Reynolds, Mark .................. 34
Rodgers, Brendan ........... 79, 93
Rogers, Wes ..................... 89
Rolison, Ryan .............. 88, 95
Rusin, Chris .................... 70
Senzatela, Antonio .............. 72
Shaw, Bryan ..................... 74
Story, Trevor ................... 36
Tapia, Raimel ................... 80
Tauchman, Mike .................. 38
Tinoco, Jesus ................... 90
Tyler, Robert .............. 90, 101
Valaika, Pat .................... 40
Vavra, Terrin ................... 89
Vilade, Ryan ............... 81, 99

Welker, Colton . . . . . . . . . . . . . . . . 82, 96     Wolters, Tony . . . . . . . . . . . . . . . . . . . . 42

Ballpark diagrams for Baseball Prospectus are created by THIRTY81Project, a design concept offering original ballpark artwork, including the new 'Ballparks of 2019' 11 x 17 color print.

Visit **www.thirty81project.com** for full details.

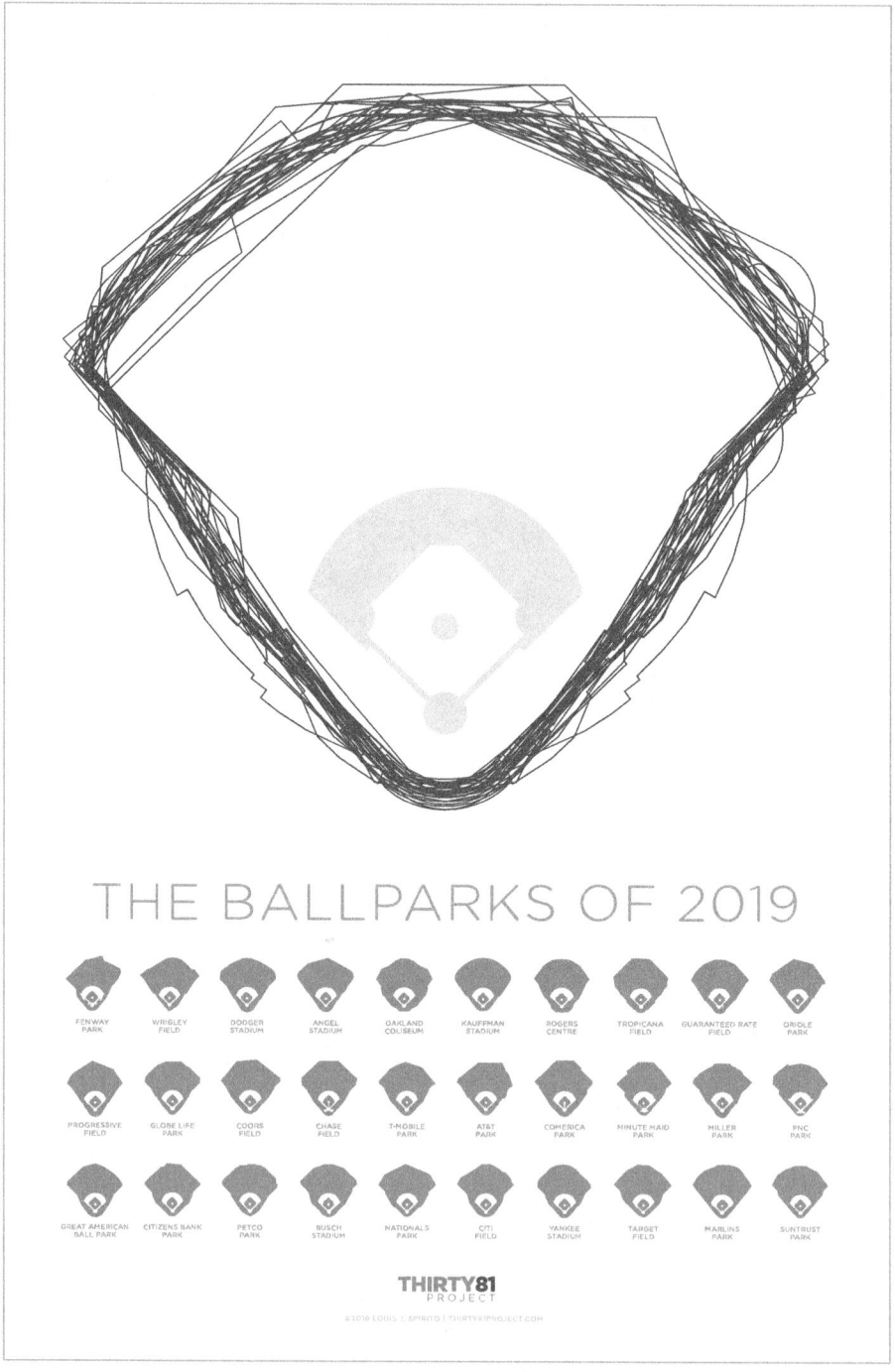